SPEED SECRETS

PROFESSIONAL RACE DRIVING TECHNIQUES

ROSS BENTLEY

MBI Publishing Company

Printed in USA

First published in 1998 by MBI Publishing Company, 729 Prospect Avenue,
PO Box 1, Osceola, WI 54020-0001 USA

MBI Publishing Company books are also available at discounts in bulk quantity
for industrial or sales-promotional use. For details write to Special Sales Manager
at Motorbooks International Wholesalers & Distributors, 729 Prospect Avenue,
PO Box 1, Osceola, WI 54020-0001 USA.

Library of Congress Cataloging-in-Publication Data
Bentley, Ross.
    Speed secrets: professional race driving techniques/Ross Bentley.
       p. cm.
    Includes index.
    ISBN 0-7603-0518 (alk. paper)
    1. Automobile racing. I. Title.
GV1029.B42   1998
796.72—dc21   98-7282

Printed in the United States of America

Contents

Acknowledgments

The most difficult part of writing this book was deciding whom to acknowledge and thank—I didn't want to leave anyone out. In reality, almost everyone with whom I've ever had contact in racing has had some influence on me, and therefore, this book. However, it would only be fair to mention a few who have made a huge impact on my life.

First, I want to thank my family for their support, encouragement, and help throughout my career. I've learned everything about commitment, fair play, and hard work from my parents, which, by the way, goes a long way in this sport. They don't know how much I appreciate that. After reading this, I hope they do.

A lot of friends have helped me and taught me much over the years. Although it's not possible to name them all, I hope they know who they are and how much I appreciate all their support. Friendships will always be the most important thing I've gained from racing.

I've learned a lot from teaching others. Thanks to all the instructors I've worked with for sharing their knowledge with me. The same goes for all the mechanics, engineers, and teams I've worked with. There is a little of each of them in this book.

A big part of this book is a result of what I've learned from Ronn Langford, my "mental coach." Through Ronn, I've learned how to maximize my own performance on a consistent basis. He is also a great friend.

I would like to single out a few people in racing who have given me a lot, including opportunities and knowledge. Tom Johnston, Dale Coyne, Craig T. Nelson, and Lee Payne—thank you all.

I've had the opportunity to work with three people in racing who are the absolute best at what they do. No one knows more about driver safety equipment than Kendall Merrill and Bell Auto Racing, and I have learned more about shock absorbers in 2 minutes from Jeff Braun than I have in the rest of my career put together. I thank both of them for their input to this book.

The third person is Michael Gue, whom I believe is the best race team manager in the business. I thank him for sharing with me just a small percentage of his knowledge.

Thanks to Craig T. Nelson, James Weaver, Dr. Brock Walker, Bruce McCaw, and Danny Sullivan for their comments and contributions throughout this book. It's an honor to have their input.

And finally, to my wife, Robin, who is my biggest supporter, fan, coach, confidante, editor . . . you name it, she does it: Thanks! Without her, we wouldn't be where we are today.

Foreword

Sometime around the beginning of the 1995 IMSA World Sports Car season, Dan Clark, team manager and co-driver of the Screaming Eagles World Sports Car team, and I were looking for a driver to share time with us in the formidable Twenty-Four Hours of Daytona. Dan sent me a tape of four drivers for review. They were drivers of varying experience, age, and monetary requirements, but they were all pros. Hot shoes. Shooters. Jockeys. They were good.

I had watched two tapes and about four minutes into the third tape I called Dan. This guy is fantastic! Look at his hands—they don't move! I thought the tape was in slow motion. There was no effort. He was smooth. He had finesse. The car he was driving was a Chevy-powered Spice, which was not a very forgiving car to say the least, and on a difficult circuit like Daytona where you must be precise, one could expect to see a driver quite active and at times anxious as he fights to control a car that is not behaving. There was no evidence of that with this driver. If anything, it was calm in that cockpit. The shifts were precise, without haste. It was tidy. He was getting the most out of a car that most drivers would find difficult at best to drive at speed. Yet he was not only smooth, he was quick.

That driver was Ross Bentley and he became my teammate, instructor, and mentor (and, on a lighter side, the "pun meister"). As a teammate, Ross shared his racing experience in so many areas. His knowledge of the nuances of the track was invaluable; he knew precisely where, if you were paying attention, you could save a tenth or even half a second.

Ross helped with it all: braking—not only how and when to apply the brakes, but more importantly as I have learned, how to come off the pedal; pacing—when to push it and when to relax and wait; car setup—a difficult subject because so much of it is related to the driver's feel (and when it's springs and shocks, you begin to think, especially if you are a rookie or novice driver, that setup is closely related to alchemy) but Ross was able to explain it all in the simplest terms; then there were tires, tires, and more tires, pressures, temperatures, wear rates, and so on; and nutrition—eat this, don't eat that, workout programs, fluid intake.

It became clear to me that this sport of auto racing was just that, a sport. Ross approached it that way and expected us to follow suit. We did and in the process I became a fan. He knows what he is talking about. I have seen him apply and share his experience with the same ease that he exhibits in the race car, and as a teammate he gave us his best all the time.

For most of 1996 and all of 1997, I had the opportunity to race against "Roscoe." He became a competitor and an adversary. Ross was driving for Jeff Jones in the Make a Wish Riley & Scott World Sports Car with Chevy power, and we had a Riley & Scott Ford-powered World Sports Car. We had horsepower. They had Ross. I have never enjoyed racing more, trying to outdo, outmuscle, and out-think Ross Bentley. I was outclassed. It took too much effort to beat a guy whose style was effortless.

Many of the valuable elements of racing that he taught me and other drivers are in this book, including 99 percent of what it takes to drive a car in competition, at speed, at the limit, driving to win, and much more. The 1 percent Ross left out is up to you. Besides that, he is a race driver. He's not gonna tell you everything. After all, he may have to race against you someday.

Craig T. Nelson
Owner/Driver, Screaming Eagles Racing
Malibu, California

Introduction

What does it really take to be a winner in auto racing? What separates the winners from the also-rans? Why do some drivers win more often than others? What can you do to become a consistent winner?

These are difficult questions to answer. Anyone who came up with a definitive solution that would work every time out would be rich!

Well, I'm not rich, nor do I claim to have all the answers. I have, however, studied the act of driving a race car for many years—as much as anyone, I think. I've instructed and coached thousands of men and women in various driving techniques. I've seen what works, and I've seen what doesn't—from the side of the track, on television, in the passenger seat, and behind the wheel.

I've spent a lot of time analyzing the techniques, styles, and actions of some of the greatest race drivers both on and off the track. I've been fortunate enough to have raced against some of them and seen them firsthand—up close and personal. I've raced wheel-to-wheel with drivers from every level of the sport. I've driven a lot of different types of race cars. That has taught me quite a bit. And, finally, I've won a few races myself.

As I said, I've learned a lot from other drivers. I've also gained a lot of knowledge from team owners, engineers, mechanics, instructors, and other friends and relatives in the sport. In fact, I've taken most of what has worked for me from watching and listening to others. I want to pass on as much of this as I can.

I've spent much of my career driving cars that were less than competitive. Not because the teams I've been with haven't been great, but because of the budget I've had to work with. Budget restrictions forced me to find my advantage in my driving and prepared me well for the occasions when I've had a competitive car.

As a result of the less-than-competitive equipment I've often raced, my results have not been as good as I would have liked. This has led some people to doubt my abilities. Personally, I've never been bothered by that. I know my capabilities, as do many of my fellow drivers and teams. The people that have doubted my abilities—and may doubt yours someday—are usually the ones who claim they could do better if they had the opportunity. Well, I've always said, please do. It's not like someone came along and handed me an Indy car. Nor is anyone going to do that for you. I've worked hard to get where I wanted to be, and you will have to do the same.

The lesson here is, judge your abilities yourself. Don't let other people tell you how much talent you have—either good or bad. In fact, listening and believing the hype about how great you are can be just as detrimental as criticism.

You've got to be hungry every step of your career. If you start believing you're so great, you may not work as hard. Like many things, a balance is the key as is being 100 percent honest with yourself.

Being a consistent race winner takes a lot more than just the skill to drive a race car quickly. A race driver needs an entire program to make him or her successful: the best car and team, the funding, a proper testing plan, and so much more.

However, once you have that program in place, to win with any regularity you must be able to drive the car at its limit consistently. That is what this book is all about.

When you analyze it, only three factors affect your ability to drive at the limit: the car, the track, and you, the driver. And typically, that's the order in which most race drivers work on being a winner. They'll spend thousands of dollars on making the car faster—trick engine parts, the latest shock absorbers, and more. They may spend hours and hours analyzing and reviewing the trick line through a corner, or where they begin braking at the end of the straight. Rarely, if ever, do they think about that last factor—the driver.

Is that the right way to look at it? I don't think so. In most cases, there is more to be gained by maximizing the performance of the driver than tricking out the car. The most important factor is the driver, the ultimate control system of a race car.

This book may be organized in the typical fashion—car first, driver last—but I am going to look at each of these areas strictly from the driver's point of view. For example, in Part 1, The Car, I won't tell you how to adjust springs or wing angles to control an oversteering car. There are many excellent race car preparation books that tell you how to do that. This is a driver's book—I'm going to tell you what you may be doing to cause that oversteer, how to identify it, and how to correct it to make you go faster.

Part 2, The Track, explains in detail how to maximize your performance by analyzing and using the track to your advantage. It covers ideal cornering lines, track surfaces, and layout, and how to deal with other drivers.

In Part 3, The Driver, I'll discuss the mental and physicals skills required to make you a winner. I believe this is the most important part of the book.

Finally, in Part 4, The Finish Line, I'll cover all the other aspects of racing that are necessary to win.

Many drivers talk about their "secret" trick line through a corner, or the "secret" demon tweak they've done to their car. I'm not so sure there are any secrets involved with winning races. Winning is usually a result of a lot of hard work, determination, motivation, skill, practice, preparation, and more. No secrets there.

I have, however, selected a few key points that some might call secrets. If you remember and use them, they will help you become a winning driver. I've highlighted them throughout the book as "Speed Secrets" (and then listed them again at the end).

After writing the first draft of this book I went back and tried to add some personal experiences that I thought might make the book a little easier to understand

and relate to. Then I asked a few friends and people I admire—1996 FIA GT World Champion James Weaver, Dr. Brock Walker of TracTec (the most knowledgeable person in the world on race car cockpit safety and design), Bruce McCaw (owner of the PacWest Indy car team), and Danny Sullivan, the 1985 Indy 500 winner and 1988 PPG Indy Car Champion—for some input. I really have to thank them; their personal comments and insights are invaluable.

Driving a race car is not something you can do "by the book." You have to learn mostly through hands-on experience. But, you can learn many of the basics by reading and studying a book. In fact, a book may allow you to learn more quickly once you're behind the wheel. If you understand the theory—if you can picture it clearly in your head before you start to drive—you will be more sensitive to and able to relate to the experience. And that means you will learn to drive at the limit much sooner. You may save years of trial-and-error learning by simply reading and understanding this book.

Racing is different from most other sports in one way: race drivers rarely have coaches. I don't really understand why (although coaches are becoming a little more common in racing). Perhaps it is due to the high cost of racing. The extra cost of a coach is seen as a waste, and most drivers would rather (wrongly) spend that money on making the car faster. Over the past few years I've had the opportunity to work as a one-on-one coach with a number of drivers. The results are always better than expected. I highly recommend using a personal driving coach if you can. Until you do—and while you do—think of this book as your coach. Use it. Don't just read it and stick it on a shelf. Keep going back to it to refresh your memory or when you are moving up a notch on the racing ladder.

For the beginner, I hope this book serves as reference material for a long time. Some of the information may not make sense until you've gone past the basics and begun working on fine-tuning your techniques. But I hope it will help you start on the right foot, and you can refer to it again later.

The experienced racer may already know a lot of the information here. You may already be using many of the techniques, although you may not understand why you are using them. I suggest you read the book anyway and really think it through. It's surprising how a fresh approach can sometimes make it all click for you, resulting in a dramatic increase in speed.

This book is written not only for the novice racer, but also for the experienced driver who has reached a plateau, or a point where he or she can't seem to go any faster. My hope is this book will do more than just teach you the basics of how to drive a race car quickly. I want to give you the ammunition and background to continue to analyze how to go faster at all times.

Most importantly, I'd like this book to teach you not only how to drive fast, but also how to be a winner in any class or level of racing.

PART 1

The Car

In this first part of the book, I will give you the basics of how to use the race car's controls to enable you to drive at the limit. I will help you understand vehicle dynamics—what the car is doing while you are driving it at its limit—and give you a fundamental knowledge of suspension and chassis functions.

Remember that I'm looking at these topics strictly as a driver. An engineer may not explain it the way I do. He would want to make sure all the technical gobbledygook was dead-on. I want to simplify it so that it makes sense to the person behind the wheel. What I'm saying is not wrong. It's just that I won't concern myself here with the exact science of it. What I care about is that you, the driver, understand it. And that you can explain it to an engineer. Most good engineers don't want a technical explanation from the driver. They want a detailed explanation of how the car feels. So, learn how to tell what the car is doing, not why. This will make you a better race driver.

Chapter 1

Behind the Wheel

If you want to drive a race car well, whether to win an Indy car race or just have fun competing in the middle of the pack in an amateur race, you must be seated properly in the car. First of all, you must be comfortable, otherwise it will be overly tiring and very difficult to concentrate. Many races have been lost simply because a driver lost concentration due to discomfort from a poorly fitted seat.

When I first started racing, I was told a seat that fits well could be worth half a second per lap. After many years of racing, I still believe this to be true. I recall two races in my career where I lost positions simply due to a seat that caused me so much pain I could not drive effectively. The first was a Trans-Am race in Portland, Oregon, where the seat bracket broke, allowing the seat to flex and move. I had to use so much effort and energy just trying to keep my body stable that I couldn't concentrate on what I was doing. The second time was in an Indy car race at Long Beach in 1993. We hadn't yet been able to build a seat that gave my lower back and hips enough support; by 30 laps into the race I had pinched a nerve in my hip, causing my right leg to go entirely numb.

The race car seat, and your position in it, is more important than most racers ever think—especially when first starting their racing career. Many drivers are so wrapped up in getting prepared for their first few races and in making the car fast that they forget to pay attention to making the seat fit properly.

Being comfortable in the car is critical. If you're not comfortable, it will not only take more physical energy to drive, but it will also affect you mentally. A painful body will reduce your concentration level.

Top drivers in Indy cars, Formula One, sports cars, and NASCAR will spend upwards of 10 hours working to make their seat fit just right, and then they fine-tune it all year long.

Dr. Brock Walker says: "The driver's body has only three points of contact with the car: the seat, the steering wheel, and the pedals. The driver's optimum postural position, contained within a proper seating system, will eventually activate the amount of control, sensitivity, strength, and general influence that the driver will possess over both the steering wheel and the pedals. Controlled smooth, efficient maneuvering inside the cockpit relates directly to consistent results and faster lap times."

You receive much of the feedback from the car through the seat. When you are sitting properly in a well-built seat you will be more sensitive to the various vibrations and g-forces you need in order to interpret what the car is doing.

You should use a seating position that puts as much of your body in contact with the car as possible. You want to sit in the seat, not on it, with as much lateral support as possible—the limiting factor being the ability to move your arms freely.

You should sit as upright as possible, with your shoulders back (not hunched forward) and your chin up. Of course, the lower you sit in the car the better. This is the most efficient way of driving a race car—it's where you are the strongest and most sensitive to the car. It's also the safest.

This seating position should allow you to turn the steering wheel 180 degrees without any interference and without moving your hands on or from the wheel. To do this, you should be able to place your hand at the top of the steering wheel (at the 12 o'clock position) and still have a bend at the elbow without pulling your shoulder off the seatback. Check this with the seatbelts/safety harness done up tight. Many drivers sit too far away from the steering wheel with their arms almost straight. This doesn't allow you the leverage to turn the steering wheel properly. It's also very tiring to drive in this position.

While seated, check to see if you can reach the shifter comfortably. You may have to modify or adjust the shifter to suit.

Dr. Brock Walker says: "The driver's posture and placement inside the cockpit dictate the seating design. All too often we see an attempt at the opposite. Driver positioning and/or seat placement should never be dictated by the steering wheel, gear shift, or pedal positioning. Always concentrate on driver placement first—then move everything else to the driver."

You should also be able to depress the pedals fully and still have a slight bend in the legs. This is not only the least tiring position but allows for ideal modulation of the pedals as you will be able to depress them by pivoting your foot at the ankle, not moving your entire leg in mid-air.

Whenever possible, I highly recommend that you have a custom-fitted seat built for you. The best way is to have Dr. Brock Walker of TracTec (or someone else who specializes in custom seat building) make one for you. However, with a little thought and preparation you can mold a seat yourself using an expandable foam. This is a simple operation, which can greatly improve your driving performance. Use a two-part foam (available at fiberglass shops) that forms up like a solid Styrofoam-type material. It is poured into a plastic bag between your body and the seat shell or monocoque tub. Before pouring, be sure to cover everything—and I mean everything!—with plastic garbage bags, as the foam is practically impossible to remove after it's set on something. Upon removing the plastic bags, you can trim off the excess and cover it with tape or material (preferably fire retardant), or you can then use it as a mold to make a carbon-fiber or fiberglass seat.

Dr. Brock Walker recalled this story: "In the spring of 1996 I stopped at Long Beach on my way to Asia, and I ran into Buddy Lazier's father, Bob. He told me that Buddy could use some help in designing a special seat for the Indy 500, which was to take place in a few weeks. 'A special seat?' I thought, 'that would be the understatement of the year!'

"A few weeks prior, Buddy had been involved in a serious accident at Phoenix. Multiple fractures in the lower spine left Buddy quite disabled. And when I say multiple—I mean multiple.

"So I went to Indianapolis to build him a seat. I decided that if I was going to participate in this venture, I would really get creative because Buddy couldn't stand, or lay down for that matter. The whole team pitched in and allowed me access to the cockpit. We kicked some butt over the course of the next few days. When we finished I was a little unsure of the project. All I knew for sure was that when I arrived Buddy couldn't rest standing, sitting, or lying; when I left the track a few days prior to the race, we would find him with his eyes closed, resting in the seat. This was a good sign, but I knew the related medical problems would probably overrule everything else. In fact, I thought that if all went well during the race, Buddy could do no more than 50 or 60 laps because he was experiencing intense, even disabling levels of pain.

"As you know, Buddy went on to win the 1996 Indianapolis 500. Data acquisition allows us to analyze and compare 1996 car and driver performance to previous Indy 500 winners. The computer will verify that Buddy Lazier would have been a hard man to beat that day, no matter who was on the track.

"Since then, much has been reported about this special seat, and it is primarily responsible for much of the attention given motorsport seating safety today. Preparation, skill, technology, and luck need to be present in order to win the 500. On this day, a special seat fit into the winning equation. As Buddy said, 'For Brock and myself, it once again proved that the seat is the most underrated piece of equipment in Indy car technology.' "

Any time you build, modify, or adjust your seat or seating position in the race shop, you have to realize it will be only on the track that you will know for sure how it feels. Every time I've had a perfect-fitting seat in the shop it has needed modifications after being used on the track. Consider this before spending a lot of time and money on covering the seat. Wait until it's been track-proven.

Speaking of covering seats, don't bother with a lot of soft padding. It will only crush and distort with the g-forces of your body against it and result in a loose-fitting seat. Besides, you need to feel the vibrations and forces from the car. Thick padding will reduce your sensitivity. If you do use padding, use only a thin layer of high-density foam rubber.

Dr. Brock Walker says: "The seat should employ varied characteristics that allow it to function as a tool; it's not just a convenient device to hold the driver in the car. This tool needs to possess measured qualities including weight, material combinations, flex, torque, and component deflection designs. In terms of direct driver benefits, we consider anatomical g-load distribution from spiked g's, sustained g's, and g's initiated by impact. Additionally, driver containment, protection, and comfort include such benefits as custom sculptured materials that support the driver under g-force conditions but simultaneously promote the driver's circulation. (The selection of materials for this application are usually based on the driver's past medical history. An example would be a driver who may have sustained leg, feet, or back injuries and needs to incorporate special support, stabilization, and circulation.) Additional considerations affecting the design, construction, and manufacturing of the seat are the driver's physical measurements, postural placement, and driving habits. Lastly, the sort of events, length of the races, and the track types greatly influence the project. When the tool is created properly, there will be dramatic improvement in driver control. The end result—faster lap times."

Use the balls of your feet on the pedals. They are the strongest part of the foot, as well as the most sensitive. When you are not using the clutch, the left foot should be on the dead pedal (the rest pad area to the left of the clutch pedal), not hovering above the clutch pedal. This will help support your body under the heavy braking and cornering forces you will experience. However, some single-seater race cars are so narrow in the pedal area that it is almost impossible to have a dead pedal. Do everything you can to make even a very small one. But if you can't, it's even more important to have a well-built seat. Ensure there is good support in front of your buttocks to stop your body from sliding forward under heavy braking.

Before getting into your car and heading out onto the track, make sure that both the pedals and the bottom of your shoes are dry and clean. Many drivers have crashed because their feet slipped off the brake pedal approaching a corner. Have a crew member wipe your shoes with a clean rag before getting into the car. I remember going to my first Formula One Grand Prix race in Montreal. It rained really hard that year. And one of the things I remember most is watching the drivers being taken to their cars on a cart, and then lifted straight from the cart into the car so that their feet wouldn't get wet. I also saw other drivers wearing plastic bags over their shoes.

The safety harnesses in a race car are not only there in case of a crash, but also to help support your body. Use only the very best seatbelts in your car, and then take good care of them. Keep them clean and inspect them often for wear and damage. Adjust them so they hold your body firmly and comfortably. And remember, they will stretch and loosen throughout the course of a race—particularly the shoulder harnesses—so ensure you can reach down and tighten them while driving (more about belts in chapter 26). Also be sure you have some form of head restraint behind your helmet.

Make sure any part of the roll cage or cockpit with which you could come in contact during a crash is covered with a high density foam rubber. Many drivers have been seriously injured just by impacting the roll cage. You might be amazed at how much a driver moves in the cockpit during a crash, even when tightly belted in. Some drivers' heads have actually made impact with the steering wheel.

And finally, do everything possible to help keep the cockpit cool. Have air ducts installed to direct air at you. The cockpit of a race car can get extremely hot, which will negatively affect your stamina and, therefore, your performance.

Chapter 2

The Controls

A race driver has a number of controls to help achieve the desired goal of driving at the limit—the steering wheel, shifter, gauges, clutch pedal, brake pedal, throttle, and even the mirrors. Everything you do with these controls should be done smoothly, gently, and with finesse.

I often see racers, particularly at the back of the pack in amateur races, trying to go fast, with their arms flailing around, banging off shifts, jerking the steering into a turn with feet stabbing at the pedals—the car usually in massive slides through the turns. It may feel fast and even look fast, but I'll guarantee it's not. In reality, the car will be unbalanced and, therefore, losing traction and actually going slower. If the driver would only slow down, the car would actually go faster. It reminds me of the saying, "never confuse movement for action."

SPEED SECRET #1:
The less you do with the controls, the less chance of error.

Steer, shift, and use the pedals smoothly, and with finesse—not with blinding speed and brute force.

SPEED SECRET #2:
The slower you move, the faster the car moves.

Gauges

A typical race car has four main gauges to which you need to pay attention if you want to drive reliably at the limit. They are: tachometer, oil pressure, oil temperature, and water temperature. Use the tach to help you go fast, and the others to help ensure the car keeps running.

You may also have to deal with other gauges such as fuel pressure, ammeter, turbo boost pressure, exhaust temperature, and so on.

It's important that the gauges are mounted so that you can see them easily and read them at a glance. Often, it is best to mount the tachometer and other gauges rotated so the range that you must see is in good view; the redline or ideal needle position should be at the 12 o'clock position. This way, with a quick glance, you know when to shift or whether the temperatures or pressures are OK.

Also, make sure the gauges don't reflect the sunlight into your eyes or have so much glare that you can't read them.

Normally, you should only have to take a quick glance at the gauges, checking more for a change of position of a needle rather than the absolute number it is pointing at.

A simple dashboard layout is best, with as few gauges as possible. More and more race cars are now using computerized dashes that are linked to data acquisition systems. These are very useful as they can tell you your lap time, your minimum or maximum speed at various points on the track, and other information that you can use to help determine where you may be able to improve. However, don't let yourself get so caught up in reading all the information that it takes away from your driving.

I like to use the tach at the exit of most corners to judge how well I did in that particular corner. It's my report card. I pick a spot on the track and check how many revs the engine is at. If I'm pulling 50 more revs than the previous lap I know what I did differently worked on that lap. Also, I try to glance at my gauges at least once a lap on the straightaway. Otherwise, I depend on the warning lights to advise me of any problems.

Warning or "idiot" lights can prove very valuable. These are usually set to come on only if one of the critical engine functions reaches an unacceptable level, such as if the oil pressure drops below 40 pounds per square inch (psi), or the water temperature reaches 240 degrees. Because these lights warn you if there is a major problem, you can check the gauges only when it's convenient, like on the straightaway.

Brake Pedal

When braking, think of "squeezing" the brake pedal down—and easing off it. The smoother you are with the brakes, the better balanced the car will be, enabling you to drive at the limit. Three-time World Driving Champion Jackie Stewart claimed one of the reasons he won so many Grand Prix was because he eased off the brakes more smoothly than any of his competitors. Hard to imagine how that could affect the outcome of a race so much, isn't it? But it allowed him to enter corners a fraction of a mile per hour faster because the car was better balanced. Obviously, this squeezing on and easing off the brake pedal must be done quickly—and it can be done very quickly with practice—but always emphasizing smoothness.

SPEED SECRET #3:
Squeeze the brake pedal on, and ease off.

This is one technique you can safely and easily practice every day on the street. Every time your foot goes onto the brake pedal, think of the word "squeeze";

think of the word "ease" when releasing the brakes. Practice it so that quickly squeezing and easing becomes second nature or habit.

Left Foot Braking

Left foot braking is a technique required when racing on oval tracks. Its use on roadracing tracks is much less frequent. In fact, most drivers never use it in road-racing, although it may have some benefits in fast turns where you're not required to downshift prior to the corner. It's also useful when driving turbocharged cars, as it allows you to stay on the throttle with the right foot, keeping the turbo spinning, and reducing the throttle lag. As you can imagine though, this is very hard on the brakes, so be careful not to overwork them.

Left foot braking saves time—time spent moving the right foot from the throttle to the brake. It also allows a smoother transition from throttle to brakes and back to throttle. But braking with the left foot takes a lot of practice to acquire the necessary sensitivity—a sensitivity you have acquired with your right foot from years of working the throttle.

By smoothly squeezing the brakes with the left foot while easing the right foot off the throttle, you can reduce the amount the car "nose-dives." This reduces the amount of weight being transferred forward, keeping the car better balanced, and resulting in more traction (more about this in chapter 5).

With left foot braking, particularly on oval tracks, some drivers make the error of having the brakes on slightly while accelerating out of a corner. This dragging of the brakes wastes time, can overheat the brakes, and is definitely unwanted. Pay attention to—and avoid—this.

Throttle

Always use the throttle (gas pedal) gently. As with the brakes, progressively squeeze on more throttle as you accelerate and quickly ease off as you slow down. Anytime you pounce on the gas pedal or abruptly lift off it unsettles the car, which reduces traction. The smoother you are with the throttle, the better balanced the car will be, and ultimately the more traction and speed you will have.

SPEED SECRET #4:
The throttle is not an on-off switch.

If you find yourself having to back off the throttle after you begin accelerating in a corner, you must have applied the gas too soon or too hard in the beginning. Ease on the throttle. It takes time and practice to develop a feel for how quickly and how much throttle you can squeeze on.

When you are moving your foot from the throttle to the brake pedal, or vice versa, it must be done as quickly as possible. Your right foot should always be either on the throttle (even if it's a light, steady throttle) or the brakes. Don't waste time doing nothing, with your foot in between the two. You should never be coasting.

Steering Wheel

Use a firm but relaxed grip on the steering wheel, with your hands in the 9 and 3 o'clock positions. Lightly hook your thumbs over the spokes of the wheel if that's comfortable. By always holding the wheel in the same position, you'll know how much you've turned it and where straight ahead is. You will see how important this is when the car begins to spin and you don't know which way is straight ahead!

With the 9-and-3 grip you should be able to steer through almost every corner without moving your hands from this position. This will result in smoother, more-controlled steering. Perhaps, in a few large, production-based racing sedans you may not be able to turn sharp enough for some very tight hairpin corners with this grip. In that case, reposition your hands slightly before the corner (e.g., to the 7 and 1 positions for a right-hand corner), to allow you to make one steering action without sliding the hands around the wheel.

When turning the steering wheel, allow both hands to do an equal amount of work. While one hand pulls down on the wheel, the other pushes up smoothly. Keep both hands on the wheel at all times (except when shifting, obviously—but even then, get your hand back on the wheel between gear changes). Make small steering corrections with the wrist, not the arms. Every wheel movement must be made smoothly and progressively, never jerking the steering into a turn. Feed in the required steering input to generate a gentle, smooth arc through the corner.

Think about it. Every time the front tires are at an angle to the road they are scrubbing off speed. Pretty obvious, right? But what does this really mean? How can you get around a corner without turning the steering wheel? Look and think further ahead, planning your path or line through a corner, so that you will be able to turn the steering as little as

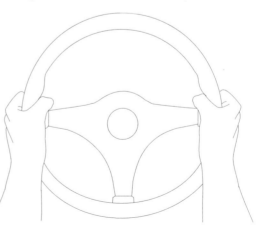

The proper hand placement on the steering wheel, at the 9 and 3 o'clock positions.

possible, straightening the corner out as much as possible. If you feel or hear the front tires scrubbing or squealing through a turn, try to unwind your steering input (straighten it out).

SPEED SECRET #5:
The less you turn the steering wheel, the faster you will go.

Once you've turned into a corner, try to unwind the steering as soon as possible. Of course, this means you have to use up all the road available. You can even practice this on the street (within limits of the law), steering smoothly into and out of corners, keeping the front wheels pointed as straight as you can.

SPEED SECRET #6:
Keep steering movement to a minimum.

Mirrors

Mirrors play a critical role in the race driver's job, and you must be comfortable using them. In racing, it is just as important to know what's behind and beside you as it is to know what's in front. Take time to adjust all your mirrors properly, and make sure they don't vibrate so much that you can't see anything in them.

You should use your mirrors enough to know who's around you at all times, and exactly where they are. A competitor should never take you by surprise by being somewhere (such as inside of you on the approach to a corner) you didn't expect.

SPEED SECRET #7:
Check your mirrors as often as it takes to always know where everyone else is around you.

However, don't constantly look in the mirrors as you drive. Some drivers have caused more problems doing that than they would have if they never looked in the mirrors. I've seen drivers veer off the track while looking in the mirrors!

I take a quick glance in the mirrors each time I come onto a straightaway of any decent length. If I adjust them properly (aimed a little to the sides so that I can see to either side), I don't actually have to turn my head to look in the mirrors to see other cars—I automatically notice them with my peripheral vision, minimizing the chances of being surprised by a faster overtaking car.

The mirrors on some modern formula cars have gotten smaller and smaller over the years. Fortunately, I think they've gotten as small as they will ever get. If you are using a small mirror, make sure it is convex to help increase your vision to the rear and sides.

Chapter 3

Shifting

Proper shifting technique is an often overlooked racing skill. Many drivers feel they have to bang off their shifts as fast as possible to go quickly. Wrong! In fact, the amount of time you can save is minimal, especially compared to the time you can lose if you miss one single shift. A shift should be made gently and with finesse.

SPEED SECRET #8:
A shift should be made gently and with finesse.

Simply place the shifter into gear as smoothly as you can. A shift should never be felt. You may be surprised at just how slowly and relaxed the world's top drivers shift.

Downshifting is one of the most misunderstood and misused techniques in driving. And it is a must for extracting the full potential of your car. It's not always easy—it requires timing, skill, and practice—but when mastered, it will help you drive at the limit.

What is the real reason for downshifting? Many drivers think it's to use the engine to help slow the car down. Wrong again! The engine is meant to increase your speed, not decrease it. In fact, by using the engine to slow the car you can actually hinder accurate brake modulation and balance. Race drivers, and good street drivers, downshift during the approach to a corner, simply to be in the proper gear, at the optimum engine rpm (revolutions per minute) range, to allow maximum acceleration out of the corner.

Again, the reason for downshifting is not to slow the car. I can't emphasize this enough. That's what brakes are for. Too many drivers try to use the engine compression braking effect to slow the car. All they really achieve is upsetting the balance of the car and hindering the braking effectiveness (if the brakes are right at the limit before locking up and then you add engine braking to the rear wheels, you will probably lock up the rear brakes), and more wear and tear on the engine. Brake first, then downshift.

SPEED SECRET #9:
Brake first—then downshift.

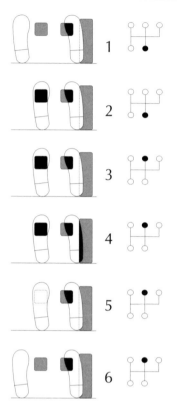

Here is a step-by-step explanation of how to heel and toe: 1. Begin braking, using the ball of your right foot on the brake pedal while keeping a small portion of the right side of your foot covering the gas pedal—but not pushing it yet. 2. Depress the clutch pedal with your left foot, while maintaining braking. 3. Move the shift lever into the next-lower gear (from fourth to third in the illustration), while maintaining braking. 4. While continuing braking and with the clutch pedal depressed, pivot or roll your right foot at the ankle, quickly pushing or "blipping" the throttle (revving the engine). 5. Quickly ease out the clutch, while maintaining braking. 6. Place your left foot back on the dead pedal, while continuing braking, now in the lower gear.

To complicate things a bit, in racing you must downshift to a lower gear while maintaining maximum braking. This must be done smoothly, without upsetting the balance of the car. But if you simply dropped a gear and let out the clutch while braking heavily, the car would nose-dive—upsetting the balance—and try to lock the driving wheels because of the extra engine compression braking effect.

The smoothest downshift occurs when the engine revs are increased by briefly applying, or stabbing, the gas pedal with your right foot. This is called "blipping" the throttle. What this does is matches the engine rpm with the driving wheels' rpm.

The tricky part is continuing maximum braking while blipping the throttle at the same time. This requires a technique called "heel and toe" downshifting. To get a basic feel for this technique, practice it while the engine is turned off (see the accompanying illustration). Then you can begin to practice it on the road or race track.

It's important to remember that you are constantly applying consistent brake pressure all the way through this maneuver. You are simply pivoting the right foot to blip the throttle while braking at the same time.

This blipping of the throttle is one of the most important aspects. You want to match the speed of the engine with the speed of the gear you are selecting. And you can't watch the tachometer—your eyes must be looking ahead. Proper blipping of the throttle and matching of revs depend on practice and input from the ears and the forces on the body. If you don't blip enough, the driving wheels will lock up when the clutch is re-engaged. That'll cause big problems! If you blip too much, the car will attempt to accelerate . . . and you are supposed to be slowing down.

The best method is to rev the engine up slightly higher than required, select the required gear, and quickly engage the clutch as the revs drop. It's going to take practice—constant practice. It may seem like a lot to do all at once, but once you get the hang of it, it will become second nature.

To heel and toe properly, your pedals must be set up correctly. When the brake pedal is fully depressed, it should still be slightly higher and directly beside the gas pedal. In a purpose-built race car, take the time to adjust the pedals to fit. If racing a production-based car, you may have to bend or add an extension to the throttle to suit you. Do not modify the brake pedal by bending or adding to the pedal. This will weaken it.

There isn't a successful race driver in the world who doesn't heel and toe on every downshift. And, again, it can be practiced every day on the street. In fact, that's the only way to drive all the time.

When I was 17 years old, I spent every last penny I had to buy my dream car—a 1969 Lotus Elan. Unfortunately, it was very well used, or should I say, abused. Anyway, I really learned a lot about driving with this car. I would go out and drive for hours and hours each day, just for fun. And as I did, I would practice shifting, particularly heel and toe downshifting. I made it my goal on each and every shift to make it perfectly smooth—so smooth that anyone in the car should not have been able to feel it whatsoever. I think this is one of the reasons why I'm easy on gearboxes today.

Now that we've talked about how to shift, what about when to shift? First, downshifting. Remember Speed Secret #9: "Brake first—then downshift." If you don't follow this rule, you will end up badly overrevving the engine.

Think about it. If you are at maximum rpm in fourth gear and you downshift to third without slowing the car, you'll over-rev the engine. And also remember downshifting is not a means of slowing the car—unless you have no brakes.

Make sure that you always complete your downshifts before you turn into a corner. One of the most common errors I've seen drivers make is trying to finish the downshift while turning into a corner. As the driver lets out the clutch (usually, without a smooth heel and toe downshift), the driving wheels try to lock up momentarily, and the car begins to spin. Time your downshift so that you have completed it, with your left foot off the clutch and over onto the dead pedal area, before you ever start to turn the steering wheel into the corner.

When upshifting, for absolute maximum acceleration you need to know the engine's torque and horsepower characteristics. With many engines you're better off shifting before reaching the redline. You want to shift at an rpm that allows the engine to stay in the peak torque range.

Let's look at an example using the "Torque & Horsepower vs. Engine RPM" graph in the accompanying illustration. Assuming a 2,000 rpm split between gears (an upshift from one gear to another dropping the engine speed by 2,000 rpm), if you shifted from first to second gear at 7,000 rpm, you would then be accelerating from 5,000 rpm back up to 7,000. As the graph shows, from 5,000 rpm the torque curve is on a decline. However, if you shifted at 6,000 rpm, the engine would be accelerating through the maximum torque range to maximum horsepower. In fact, an engine will operate most effectively—resulting in the maximum acceleration—when the rpm is maintained between the torque peak and horsepower peak.

Notice I talk more about the engine torque than horsepower. As they say, "horsepower sells cars, torque wins races." Torque is what makes the car accelerate, horsepower maintains that.

Talk to your engine builder, or study the engine dyno torque and horsepower graphs to determine the rpm at which you should be shifting. It makes a huge difference.

When you are proficient at very smooth, well-timed downshifts, try skipping gears when downshifting. Instead of running through all the gears (for example, from fifth to fourth, fourth to third, and third to second), shift directly to the required gear (from fifth to second). Obviously, this takes the right timing, using the brakes to slow the car, then downshifting just before turning into the corner. You must slow the car down with the brakes even more before dropping the two gears.

This goes back to what I was getting at earlier—the less you do behind the wheel, the faster you will go. Every time you shift, there is a chance you may make a small error that will upset the balance of the car. Shift as little as possible. In fact, the less downshifting you do while approaching a corner, the less likely it is you will make a mistake, and it will be easier to modulate the brakes smoothly.

Now, with some cars, it seems the gearbox doesn't like it when you skip gears.

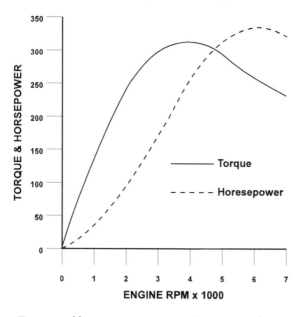

Often, it is difficult to get a perfect match of the revs, therefore making it hard to get a good, clean downshift without "crunching" it into gear. Obviously, with this type of car, you're better off not skipping gears.

What about double-clutching? I believe double-clutching is unnecessary in any modern production car (anything built in the last 15 to 20 years or so), but may be useful in some real race cars with racing gearboxes.

What is double-clutching? Basically, you depress and release the clutch twice

Torque and horsepower versus engine rpm graph.

for each shift. The routine goes like this for a downshift: you are traveling along in fourth gear and begin to slow down for a corner. You then depress the clutch pedal, move the shifter into neutral, release the clutch, rev the engine (blipping the throttle using the heel and toe method), depress the clutch again, move the shifter into third gear, and release the clutch. Your downshift is now complete.

The reason for double-clutching is to help evenly match the rpms of the gear you are selecting with that of the engine to allow a smoother meshing of the gears. In a nonsynchromesh transmission, such as a racing gearbox, it may make gear changing easier. And that's why I say it may be unnecessary to double-clutch in production-based race cars with their synchromesh transmissions. But, if the synchros in your car's transmission are beginning to wear out, double-clutching can extend their life a little longer and make it easier to get it into gear.

You may be able to go racing for many years and never have to double-clutch. But, a complete race driver knows how to, and is proficient at it. In endurance races, a driver may want to double-clutch to save wear and tear on the gearbox. At other times it is more a matter of driver preference.

Another option with a pure racing gearbox is not to use the clutch at all when shifting. This takes practice, as it is more critical that the engine and gearbox revs are matched perfectly when downshifting. The advantage to not using the clutch is that it may save a fraction of a second on each shift. The disadvantage is that it usually causes a little extra strain on the gearbox, perhaps wearing it out a little sooner or risking a mechanical failure in the race. Also, there may be more chance for you to make an error this way. Again, I think its important for a driver to know how to drive without the clutch—you never know when you're going to have a clutch problem and be forced to not use it.

More and more race cars are being built with sequential shifters. This is very much like a motorcycle shifter, in that the shift lever is always in the same position. You simply click it back to shift up, and forward to shift down. With this type of shifter it is impossible to skip gears on a downshift—you have to go through all the gears. Also, it may work better if you do not use the clutch. On an upshift, you just ease up on the throttle (as you would with a normal gearbox), and click the shifter back into the next gear. On a downshift, it works the same way only you heel and toe blip the throttle as you click it down a gear.

Throughout my career, with most cars, I have usually used the clutch when shifting—single-clutching in sprint races and double-clutching in endurance events. I've found it puts less wear and tear on the gearbox. But when I started driving cars with sequential gearboxes, I found they shifted much quicker and easier without using the clutch. It took a few laps to get used to not using it—and to not being able to skip gears on downshifts—but once comfortable with it, I realized it was the only way to go with the sequential shifter. With a regular gearbox, though, I still prefer to use the clutch.

Chapter 4

Chassis and Suspension Basics

Understanding chassis and suspension adjustments and what they mean to you as a driver is a critical part of your job. There are many good books that deal with race car dynamics in great detail. In Appendix B, I've listed the ones I think are mandatory reading for any driver.

If you don't understand something, go back to these books or ask someone to explain it. If you want to win, you must know this information.

I don't intend to go into great detail, but the following is a brief overview of some of the key areas of chassis and suspension adjustments that I feel you have to know to reach any level of success. I really hope this piques your interest to go out and learn more.

Camber

Camber angle is the inclination of the wheels looking from the front or rear of the car. A wheel inclined inward at the top is said to have "negative camber"; a wheel inclined outward at the top has "positive camber." The angle is measured in degrees.

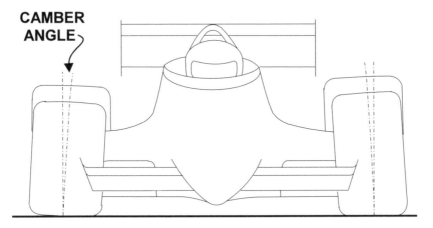

Camber is the angle of inclination of the wheels when viewed from the front or rear, and showing negative camber in this case.

It is important to keep the entire tread width of a tire—which is generally very wide and flat—in complete contact with the track surface as much as possible. When a tire is leaned over, part of the tread is no longer in contact with the track, drastically reducing traction. Therefore, the suspension must be designed and adjusted to keep the tire flat on the track surface during suspension movement.

Understand that as a car is driven through a corner, it leans toward the outside of the turn. This causes the outside tire to lean outward—more positive camber—while the inside wheel tends toward more negative camber. Therefore, to keep the outside tire (as it's the one that is generating most of the cornering force) as flat on the road surface as possible, generally the suspension is adjusted to measure negative camber when at rest or driving down a straightaway.

Your goal in adjusting the camber angle is to maximize cornering grip by having the tire close to 0 degree camber during hard cornering. This can take a fair bit of adjusting and testing to come to the best static setting that will result in the optimum dynamic camber angle.

Castor

Castor angle provides the self-centering effect of the steering (the tendency for the car to steer straight ahead without holding the steering wheel). It is the inclination angle of the kingpin, or upright, looking from the side. Positive castor is when the top of the kingpin/upright is inclined to the rear. Negative castor is never used.

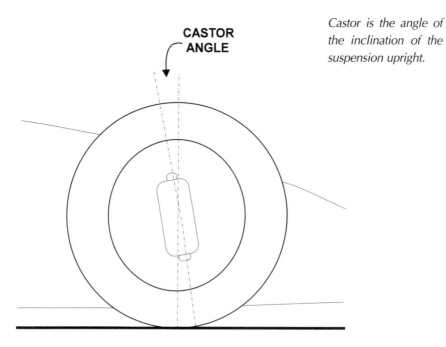

CASTOR ANGLE

Castor is the angle of the inclination of the suspension upright.

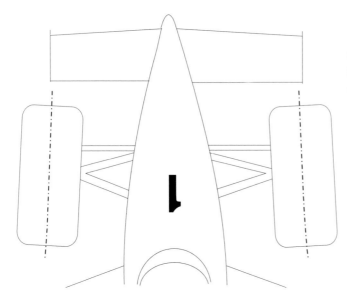

Toe is the angle of the wheels looking from above; in this case, toe-in.

The more positive castor, the more the steering will self-center—which, generally, is a desirable effect. However, the more positive castor, the more effort it takes to turn the steering against this castor. There has to be a compromise between easy self-centering and heavy steering.

Castor also affects the camber when the steering is turned. The more positive castor, the more negative camber on the outside tire during cornering. This must be kept in mind when adjusting for the optimum camber setting. Perhaps, instead of dialing in more static camber, you may be better off adjusting in more castor. Remember, this will result in more negative camber on the outside tire during cornering. This can be an important factor. Learn and understand castor.

Toe

Toe can be either "toe-in" or "toe-out." It is the angle of either the two front or two rear tires looking at them from above. Toe-in is when the front of the tires are closer together than the rear; toe-out is the opposite—the front of the tires are farther apart then the rear. Toe can always be adjusted at the front, and can be adjusted at the rear on cars with independent rear suspension.

Toe plays an important role in the car's straight-line stability, as well as its transient handling characteristics—how quickly the car responds to the initial turn into the corner. Generally, front wheel toe-in results in an initial understeer; toe-out results in an initial oversteer (more about understeer and oversteer in the next chapter).

Rear wheel toe-out must be avoided—it causes instability and an unpredictable oversteer.

Ackerman Steering

The inside wheel of a vehicle driving through a corner travels on a tighter radius than the outside wheel. Therefore, the inside front wheel must be turned sharper to avoid it scrubbing. The geometry of the front suspension is designed to achieve this. This is called Ackerman steering.

Some race cars have been designed, or modified, to have anti-Ackerman steering. This means the inside tire is actually turned less than the outside tire. The reasoning is that the inside tire has so little of the cornering load that some tire scrub will not hurt. Other cars have increased Ackerman geometry to the point where the inside wheel is turned more than would be necessary to track the inside radius. Both of these variations are designed to help the car's initial "turn-in" characteristics.

Bump Steer

Bump steer should be avoided. This is when the front or rear wheels begin to either toe-in or toe-out during the vertical suspension movements caused by a bump or from body roll (sometimes called roll steer). Although it has been used to help band-aid a handling problem, bump steer generally makes a vehicle very unstable, particularly on the rear wheels.

Antidive

When you apply the brakes, the front end of the car has a tendency to dive. The suspension geometry is designed in such a way as to reduce this tendency. Generally, this is something designed into the car and requires—or even allows— little or no adjustment.

Antisquat

When a car accelerates, the rear tends to squat down. As with antidive, the suspension geometry is designed to limit this. And again, very little adjustment is required or available.

Ride Height

The ride height is the distance between the road surface and the lowest point on the car. Often, this is different at the front than at the rear. This difference is called "rake"—usually with the front lower than the rear. Adjustment of the ride height, particularly the rake, is used to tune the handling.

The ride height is usually determined by running the car as low as possible without the chassis bottoming out (or, at least, just barely touching) on the road surface, or the suspension running out of travel. Usually, the lower the car is run, the better the aerodynamics; as well, the lower center of gravity is advantageous.

Spring Rate

The spring rate is the amount of force needed to deflect a spring a given amount, and is usually measured in pounds per inch of deflection. The diameter of the spring wire, the overall diameter of the spring, and the length or number of coils determine this rating.

Choosing the optimum spring rate is one of the most important setup factors you'll have to deal with. It's your goal in developing the car to find the optimum spring rate for the front and rear suspension. Generally, it's a compromise between having a soft enough spring to allow the suspension to handle the undulations in the track surface, while being stiff enough to keep the car from bottoming out when hitting a bump. There are many more factors involved such as your driving style or preference, the amount of aerodynamic downforce you are running, the weight of the car, the shape and condition of the track surface, and so on. Perhaps most important, though, is the balance front to rear. Generally, it's best to use the softest spring possible on the rear—to help the rear tires achieve maximum traction under acceleration—then balance the handling with the optimum front springs.

Wheel Rate

The wheel rate is the amount of force needed to move the wheel a given amount, and is also measured in pounds per inch of deflection. It is determined by the geometry of the suspension and spring mounting location, and the spring rate. Understand that even though you have the same spring rate on the front and rear suspension (or two different cars), the wheel rate may differ due to the amount of leverage a suspension system applies to the spring.

Antiroll Bar

An antiroll bar (sometimes wrongly referred to as a sway bar) is used to resist the vehicle's tendency to lean during cornering. The antiroll bar, usually a steel tube or solid bar, is used to alter the front or rear roll resistance, affecting the car's handling characteristics. Many cars have adjustment controls in the cockpit, so that you can compensate for changes in track conditions, fuel load, and tire wear during a race.

Adjusting the antiroll bars is probably the easiest and quickest change you can make to the suspension setup. Therefore it's important to try the car at full stiff and full soft settings to see what effect it has. As a general rule, to improve the grip on the front of the car (to lessen understeer), you should soften the front bar or stiffen the rear bar. To improve grip on the rear (lessen oversteer), you should soften the rear bar or stiffen the front bar. However, that's not always the case—as I've discovered a few times—so be prepared to try the opposite.

When beginning to dial in the setup of the car, I like to do a "bar sweep." This is where I will adjust the front bar from full soft to full hard; then do the same with the rear bar, while noting the change in handling. That gives my engineer and me a good indication as to which direction we will have to go to develop a good balance in the car.

Roll Stiffness

Roll stiffness is the total amount of resistance to the car leaning or rolling provided by the springs and antiroll bars. This is measured in pounds per inch of spring travel at the wheel. This is primarily a function of the spring rate and the antiroll bar stiffness.

The distribution of the vehicle's roll stiffness between the front and rear suspension is called the roll stiffness distribution and is expressed as a percentage front to rear.

Generally, it's the roll stiffness distribution that we use to fine-tune the handling balance of the car, using the springs and antiroll bars. Adjusting the front roll stiffness (with springs or antiroll bars) in relation to the rear, and vice versa, is the most common method of altering the handling balance of the car.

Shock Rate

The purpose of a shock absorber is to slow down and control the oscillations of the spring as the suspension absorbs undulations in the roadway. Actually, a shock absorber is a damper—it dampens the movement of the springs.

Shocks work in both directions: compression being called bump; extension called rebound. A shock absorber, therefore, is rated by the rate of deflection at a given shaft speed, both in the bump and rebound direction. If the car's springs are force sensitive, the shocks are velocity sensitive.

You can also use the shock absorbers to alter the transient handling characteristics—how responsive the car is to your inputs. If the springs and antiroll bars determine the amount of body roll and the distribution front to rear, then the shock absorber rates determine how quickly that body roll occurs.

During the 1993 Indy Car season, we struggled with an understeer problem with the car. At practically every race, the car would understeer in the early part of the corner—after I initially turned into the corner, but before I could get back on the throttle. At Portland we realized that as I braked for a corner and the car's front end was heavily loaded, it would turn in very well. But as I eased off the brakes it would begin to understeer. We ended up increasing the front shocks' stiffness, both bump and rebound. This would help control the amount of nose-diving the car did under braking and then stop the front end from lifting back up so quickly as I eased off the brakes entering the corner. As it turned out, this didn't solve all our problems, but it was an improvement.

So, the shock absorbers are another important suspension tuning component. And, as with the spring rate, finding the optimum shock setting is a delicate compromise. It takes some experience before you have the sensitivity as a driver to be able to find that perfect setting.

Corner Weight

If you place the four tires of a vehicle on four separate scales, they will give you the corner weights of the vehicle. From there, you can determine the front-to-rear and left-to-right weight distribution, as well as total vehicle weight.

Ideally, for a road course, the left-to-right corner weights should be identical;

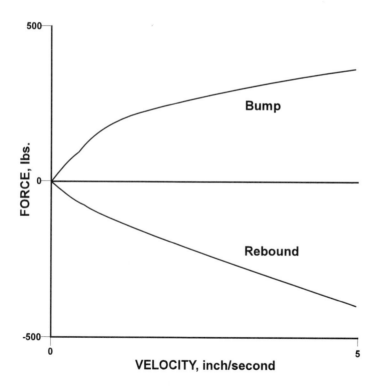

A shock absorber dyno produces a graph that relates the force it takes to stroke the shock, in both bump and rebound, versus the velocity at which it moves. Learn to read and understand shock dyno graphs and especially how their data relate to what you feel as a driver.

with practically any midengine car, the rear corner weights will be higher than the front. For oval tracks, the setup will often be biased to one side or corner.

Adjusting corner weights is one of the most important suspension tuning tools—one that is often overlooked by many inexperienced racers.

Tires

One of the most effective ways of checking and optimizing chassis adjustments is by "reading" the tires. Evaluating tire temperatures will indicate if the tire pressures are correct, if the alignment settings are correct, how the overall handling balance of the car is, and, to some extent, how close to the limit you're driving.

All tires are designed to operate within an optimum tread temperature range. In this optimum range the tire generates its maximum traction (as shown in the accompanying illustration). Above or below that optimum range, the tires will not grip the track surface well. Also, if they are operated above the optimum range for too long, the tread may begin to blister, chunk, or wear quickly. An average temperature range for a high-performance street radial is in the 180 to 200 degrees Fahrenheit area; for a racing tire, 200 to 230 degrees Fahrenheit.

To determine tire temperatures you use a tire pyrometer, an instrument with a needle that is inserted just under the surface of the tire's tread, generally at three points across the tire—the inside, the middle, and the outside of the tread.

Tire temperatures taken after the car has come into the pits are an average of the corners and straightaways. If it's after a long straightaway or a slow cool-off lap, the temperatures may be misleading as part of the tread may have cooled more than others. It's important to take temperatures as close to a corner as possible. They must also be taken as soon as the car has come to a stop as they will begin to cool after about a minute.

The optimum camber angle is indicated when the temperature near the outside of the tread is even with the temperature near the inside of the tread. If the temperature near the inside of the tread surface is significantly higher than the outside, there is too much negative camber—the inside is heating up too much. If the outside temperature is hotter than the inside, there is too much positive camber.

If the temperature in the middle of the tread is equal to the average of the inside and outside of the tread, then the tire pressure is correct. If it's too hot in the middle of the tread, then the tire pressure is probably too high; too cool in the middle and the pressures are too low. Ideally, the tire temperatures should be even all across the tread.

And if the temperatures on the front tires are even with the rear tires, then the overall balance of the car is good. If the fronts are hotter than the rears, then the

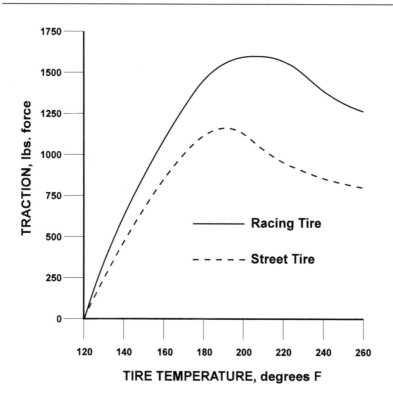

Tire temperature versus traction graph.

fronts are sliding more than the rears, and a spring, shock, or antiroll bar adjustment may be necessary. The reverse is true as well.

If all four tires are not running in the optimum temperature range, it means one of two things: either the tire compound is not correct for the application, or it has something to do with your driving. If the temperature is too low, you're not driving the car hard enough—you're not working the tires. If the temperature is too hot, you're driving too hard—you're sliding the car too much. More about this in the next chapter.

Get used to reading a tire. If you can look at the tread surface in relation to the tire temperatures and how the car felt and then determine what to do to make improvements, it may make the difference between you and your competitors.

The surface should be a very dull black all across the tread. There should not be any shiny areas. If there is, it probably means that part of the tire is being overloaded. Also, if you are driving the car hard enough—using the tires—the tread surface will show a very slight wavy grained texture. It should be this same texture all across the tread.

A couple of notes on how to treat new tires. When starting with a new set of tires, it is best to break them in. First "scrub" them in by weaving back and forth (if safely possible) to clean the mold release agent off the surface. And second, don't destroy them on the first lap by putting the car in huge slides through the corners and getting massive wheelspin under acceleration. Instead, gradually build up the heat in them by progressively increasing your speed. Their overall grip will last longer this way.

Chapter 5

Race Car Dynamics

The more you understand about the car, the more successful you will be. Take the time to learn and fully understand everything you can about how the car works, how it is set up, and what each change should do and actually does. Even if you don't work on the car yourself, being able to communicate what the car is doing to your mechanic or engineer is the only way to get the maximum performance from the car. As with many other aspects of racing, read, listen, and learn as much as you can. In Appendix B, I've listed some additional books I strongly suggest you read.

Before making vast changes to the car's setup, be sure that you first know the track well, are comfortable with it, and are driving well. I've seen drivers (myself included) get so caught up in the idea of making the car work better, they forget about their own driving (more about this in Part 3). Also, when making changes to the setup, only make one adjustment at a time. If you make more than one, how do you know which one made the difference?

I bought my first Formula Ford from a driver who had been racing for a number of years, and whom I knew was very knowledgeable about the setup and mechanics of the car. I knew the car was pretty good. So I decided I wouldn't try to out-trick myself. I promised myself I wouldn't make any drastic changes in the car for at least the first season. I was just going to concentrate on getting 100 percent out of the car as a driver, and only fine-tune the suspension. The second year I raced it, I made some serious modifications to the car; by that time I felt like I knew enough to do that.

Tire Traction

In the last chapter we looked at the tires from the perspective of how they relate to chassis adjustments. Now, let's get back to how to drive them. In fact, to get the most from your tires, you really do have to understand them. You can be somewhat successful in racing without knowing many of the suspension basics I talked about previously, but you must understand how tires work.

SPEED SECRET #10:
You will never win a race without understanding how tires work.

Every force that affects your car, and your performance, is transmitted through the four tires. Absolutely everything. So you better know how they work and be sensitive to them.

Only three factors determine the amount of traction you have available from the tires. The first is the coefficient of friction between the tire and the track surface, which is determined by the road surface itself and the rubber compound of the tire. The second is the size of the surface of the tire that contacts the track surface—the contact patch. Obviously, the more rubber in contact with the road surface, the more traction available. And the third is the vertical load on the tires. This load comes from the weight of the vehicle and the aerodynamic downforce on the tires.

Tires do not reach their limit of traction, and then all of a sudden break away into the land of skidding and sliding. Sometimes it may feel like that, but they always give you some warning signs. As they reach their adhesion or traction limit, they gradually relax their grip on the road.

In fact, primarily due to the elasticity of the rubber, tires have to slip a certain amount to achieve maximum traction. The term used to describe this tire slippage in cornering (lateral acceleration) is called "slip angle" and is measured in degrees. As your cornering forces and speed increase, the tire ends up pointing in a slightly different direction than the wheel is actually pointing. The angle between the direction the tire is pointing and the path the wheel is following is the slip angle (see the accompanying illustration).

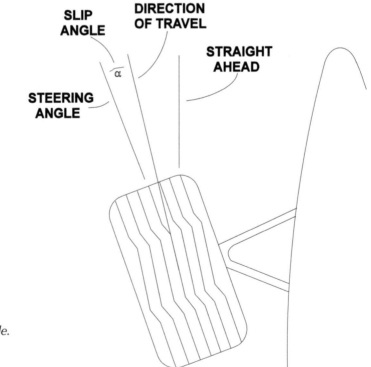

SLIP ANGLE

DIRECTION OF TRAVEL

STRAIGHT AHEAD

STEERING ANGLE

α

Tire slip angle.

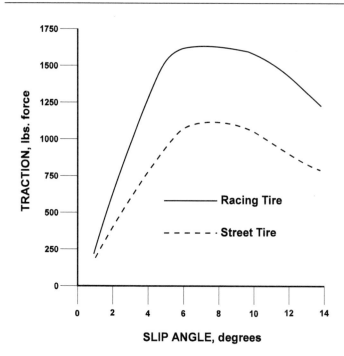

Slip angle versus traction graph.

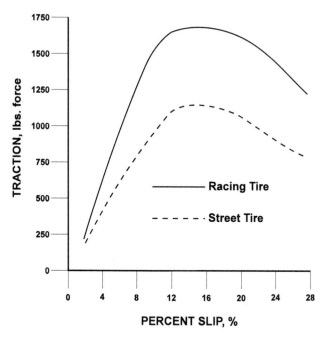

Percent slip versus traction graph.

When accelerating or braking, the amount of tire slippage is measured as a percentage.

The tire's traction limit, and therefore its cornering limit, is achieved within an optimum slip angle range, as shown by the accompanying "Slip Angle vs. Traction" graph. That range may vary slightly for different tires (radial tires slip less than bias-ply tires), but the basic characteristics remain the same. Up until that optimum slip angle range is reached, the tire is not generating its maximum traction capabilities. If the cornering speed or steering angle is increased, slip angle will increase along with tire traction until it reaches a point where tire traction then begins to decrease again.

How quickly the tire reaches its optimum range and then tapers off determines the "progressivity" of the tire. A tire that is too progressive (one that takes too long to reach its limit and then tapers off very slowly) is not responsive enough—it feels sloppy. A tire that is not progressive enough will not give the driver enough warning when it has reached its traction limit and is about to go beyond it—it doesn't have enough feel. This tire is difficult to drive at the limit since you never know precisely when you're going beyond it.

Typically, a street tire is more progressive than a racing tire. A racing tire is less forgiving than a street tire.

On a dry track, maximum traction—and, therefore, maximum acceleration, braking, and cornering (maximum slip angle)—occurs when there is approximately 3 to 10 percent slippage (as shown in the accompanying graph, "Percent Slip vs. Traction"), depending on the type of tire. This means a tire develops the most grip when there is actually a certain amount of slippage.

Fortunately, as I said earlier, when tires reach their traction limit and then go beyond, they don't lose grip completely, nor immediately. They actually lose grip progressively. And even when they are beyond the limit, completely sliding, they still have some traction.

Think about it: Even when you have locked up the brakes and you are skidding, you still slow down—not as fast as when the tires are still rotating, slipping 3 to 10 percent—but you do slow down. The same thing applies during cornering. When the car starts to slide, the tires are still trying to grip the road. And, as they grip the road they are scrubbing off speed down to the point where the tires can achieve maximum traction once again.

This is a reassuring fact to remember—it's possible to go slightly beyond the limit without losing complete control and crashing. We'll talk more about driving at and beyond the limit later in the chapter.

Acceleration

When accelerating, think of squeezing the gas pedal—don't pounce on it. Again, the throttle is not an on-off switch. It should be used progressively; squeeze it down and ease off it. This must be done quickly, but smoothly.

As I said before, there is a limit to your tire's traction—approximately 3 to 10 percent slippage on dry pavement, and somewhat less on wet pavement. Should the tires exceed this percentage of slippage, leading to wheelspin, it will result in less than maximum acceleration. At that point, simply ease off the throttle slightly, and "feather" it until you have controlled traction and maximum acceleration again.

Braking

The braking system on most race cars is more powerful than any other system in the car. In other words, the car is capable of stopping much quicker than it can accelerate. Take full advantage of this.

As with acceleration, maximum braking occurs with approximately 3 to 10 percent slippage. This means the wheels are actually turning slightly slower—3 to 10 percent slower—than they should be for any given car speed. Exceeding this limit leads to lock-up—100 percent slippage—and loss of steering control. Braking at the limit or threshold of traction is called "threshold braking." It's the fastest, most-controlled way to slow or stop a vehicle. This is what I mean by maximum braking.

Proper braking actually starts with how you take your foot off the throttle. As I mentioned earlier, do not lift off the gas pedal abruptly, but gently ease off the throttle—quickly! Then begin squeezing on the brakes, until you are at maximum braking—threshold braking. If you exceed the limit for threshold braking and begin to lock up, ease up slightly on the pedal; think of curling your toes back, feeling for the tires to begin rotating at the limit of traction again. In other words, you may have to modulate the pedal pressure slightly, using the feedback from the tire noise, the forces on your body, and the balance of the car to achieve maximum braking.

When approaching a corner, squeeze the brakes on smoothly, firmly, and progressively. Then, as you reach the corner, release the brake pedal very gently as your foot goes to the throttle, so that you don't actually feel the point at which the brakes are fully released. Remember, in chapter 2, I mentioned what made Jackie Stewart so successful. It was how he eased off the brakes.

If you brake too hard and lock up the front wheels, you will lose all steering control. If this happens, you will have to ease your foot off the brake pedal slightly to regain control—back to threshold braking. And if you do this, you will most likely "flat-spot" the tires. This happens when the tires have skidded along the roadway and worn a patch of tire to the point where the tire is no longer perfectly round. You'll know exactly when you've done this—you'll feel a thumping or vibration in the car as the flat spot rotates.

Practice braking when driving on the street. See if you can modulate the brakes so that you can't feel the exact point where the car comes to a complete stop. Work on developing a real feel for the brakes; a very sensitive touch is important, especially in poor traction conditions.

You must be consistent with your braking. Some drivers brake hard at the beginning and then gradually ease off slightly. Others do the exact opposite: they gradually begin braking and then increase pressure throughout the braking area. The real key is to apply the same consistent hard braking all the way through the braking area.

1996 FIA GT World Champion James Weaver described it this way:

"How you depress the brake pedal, particularly as regards initial application, depends on a number of things. All else being equal, the two things that have the most influence are the type of brake pad material and the amount of aerodynamic download the car is running. If you have a lot of rear wing in the car, you can apply the brakes very hard—especially at high speed. If the car doesn't stop very well, the first thing to do is increase the rear wing. If it all goes wrong under braking and you don't have any confidence in the car, you will never be able to present the car to the corner properly. This then makes it almost impossible to get the car to turn consistently and onto the apex as you would like. Get the braking right, then work on the turn-in.

"Brake pad materials vary enormously. For roadracing, you need a pad with excellent initial bite, with good modulation and release. Some pads seem to 'self servo' and give the impression of either being 'rubbing speed' sensitive or too temperature-sensitive—when you first apply the brake, nothing seems to happen and then as the car slows down, the brakes seem to get better and better and you have to start reducing pedal pressure. This makes the car very difficult to drive.

"As regards sports car racing, look for a pad with a wide temperature operating range, good initial bite, and one that is not too aggressive on the discs. At most race meetings, there is very little practice time, so you don't want to waste time with a super sensitive pad that requires a lot of messing around with brake duct blanking, and consequently the balance."

Anti-Lock Braking Systems

I believe anti-lock braking systems (ABS) are perhaps the most important safety device to ever be developed for street vehicles. However, as of this writing, ABS has not found much use on purpose-built race cars (Indy, Formula One, IMSA GTP/WSC, Trans-Am, etc.). Why? Well, mainly because of the rules. All of these series prohibit the use of ABS, mainly as a cost-controlling measure. About the only use it saw in purpose-built race cars was in Formula One, where a couple of teams used it in 1992 and 1993. No verdict was reached on whether it was a major advantage or a disadvantage. It was banned from the 1994 season on.

However, when ABS is standard equipment on a production car, it is used on production-based race cars such as the showroom stock class. Here, ABS can be both an advantage and a disadvantage. It is a wonderful safety device, stopping a driver from ever being able to lock up the brakes. This is particularly useful in endurance racing where it's more important to be consistent and never flat-spot a tire.

At the same time, ABS can be difficult to get used to and may be even a disadvantage in racing. Often, a driver wants to "pitch" a car into a turn by going slightly beyond the threshold of traction on the rear wheels while turning into the corner. With ABS, however, this is not possible.

I once spent a couple of days testing a showroom stock Corvette. The first day it was dry, the second day it rained. Each day we ran with and without the ABS activated. In the dry I was half a second a lap quicker with the ABS turned off. The next day, in the rain, I was over a second quicker with the ABS on. I really learned the pros and cons of ABS during those two days.

It's important, if you're going to race a car with ABS, to get very comfortable with the feel of it. Get used to the feeling of the brake pedal pulsing and the inability to pitch the car into a turn with the brakes, as well as how hard you can—and have to—press the brake pedal.

Slip Angle

Let's take a closer look at slip angles. If you noticed in the "Slip Angle vs. Traction" graph, the peak traction limit, or lateral acceleration, is when the tires are in the range of 6 to 10 degrees of slip angle. Let's look at four hypothetical drivers to see where on the graph it's best to drive.

Our first driver is probably inexperienced, and definitely a little conservative. He consistently drives through the corners with the tires in the 2- to 5-degree slip angle range. As you can see from the graph, the tires are not at their maximum traction limit. Driver 1 is not driving at the limit, and therefore will be slow.

Driver 2 has a bit more experience and is known to be a little on the wild side. He consistently overdrives the car. But what does that mean? Well, he always drives through the corners with a slip angle above 10 degrees. In other words, he is sliding the car too much. It may look great, with the car in a big slide all the way through the corner, but the graph shows that in this range, the traction limit of the tires has begun to decrease from maximum. Plus, all this sliding about will increase the temperature of the tires to the point where they are overheated, further reducing the traction capabilities of the tires.

Our final two drivers are consistently cornering in the 6- to 10-degree slip angle range. Both are very fast. Both are cornering at about the same speed. Both are driving the car with the tires at the limit. So, what's the difference? Driver 3 is cornering in the upper end of the 6- to 10-degree range—about 9 or 10—while Driver 4 is around 6 or 7 degrees. Again, the cornering speed is the same, but Driver 3 is sliding a little more than Driver 4, causing more heat buildup in the tires.

Both drivers will run at the front of the pack early in the race, but eventually Driver 3's tires will overheat and he will fade. He's the one complaining at the end of the race about his "tires going off." Meanwhile, our winner—Driver 4—has gone on, consistently driving with the tires in the 6- or 7-degree slip angle range, and is praising the tire manufacturer for making a "great tire" and his crew for a "great handling car."

The goal, as this example demonstrates, is to drive consistently at the lowest possible slip angle that maintains maximum traction.

And understand that the difference in speed between cornering with a slip angle of 2 degrees and 12 degrees may be 1 or 2 miles per hour—or even less. You can imagine how much skill, precision, and practice it takes to be able to control the car well enough to stay between 6 and 7 degrees of slip angle!

SPEED SECRET #11:
Drive at the lowest possible slip angle that maintains maximum traction.

Now, I'm going to contradict myself. Sometimes you have to drive in the upper end of the ideal slip angle range. If the tires are too hard a compound for your car (perhaps they were designed for another type of car), or the track temperature is very low, you may have a difficult time getting the tires to their optimum temperature range. In this case, you may want to slide the car a little more, drive in the upper end of the optimum slip angle range to generate more heat in the tires to achieve maximum traction. The consistent winner has learned to feel this and interpret his or her tire temperature readings, then adapt his or her driving style to suit.

James Weaver put it this way: "In setting the car up, I work on the tires' average grip, not peak grip. You always drive to the car's minimum grip level—you will go faster by raising the minimum grip level. This is the best policy for a race setup. In qualifying, you can sometimes 'magic' a lap by changing the car to make it nervous and turn into the corners very quickly. In this situation, you are taking advantage of the new tire grip (i.e., peak grip) to get you into the corners as fast as possible and then just hanging on through the rest of the corner."

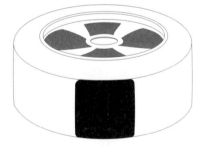

Tire Contact Patch

I really want you to understand tire contact patch, as it is the basis for much of what we'll be talking about for a while— and understanding it will allow you to dri-

The tire contact patch, or "footprint," is the part of the tire that makes contact with the track surface as it rotates.

ve at the limit. There are only four small tire contact patches (the actual patch of tire, or footprint, that is in contact with the road at any one particular time) that are actually holding you and your car on the road. The larger the contact patch, the more grip or traction a tire has. Increasing the tires' width obviously puts more tire footprint on the road. The result? More traction. Unfortunately, tire size on race cars is usually limited by the rules.

Vertical Load

Vertical load, or pressure applied downward on the tire, is not limited by the rule book, but it has a great effect on the tire contact patch and the traction it offers. By increasing this load on a tire, you increase the pressure applied on the contact patch, and thus (up to a certain point where the tire becomes overloaded) the traction limit of the tire.

Now, before you get any ideas of adding a 2,000-pound lead weight to your car, believing that the extra load will put more pressure on the tires and give them more traction, think about this: Yes, the extra load increases the traction capabilities of the tire, but the work required by the tires to grip the road while carrying that

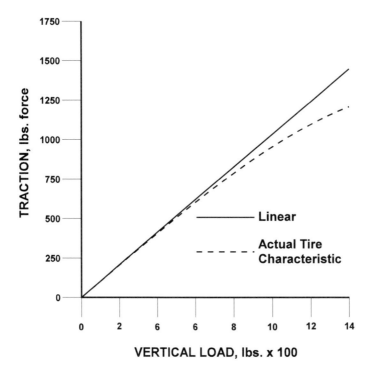

Vertical load versus traction graph.

extra load also increases. In fact, it increases even faster. It's not a linear relationship (as shown in the vertical load vs. traction graph).

So, traction increases with an increase in vertical load, but the work required of the tire increases faster. The result is an overall decrease in lateral acceleration and, therefore, cornering capabilities. This is, generally speaking, why a lighter car will handle better than a heavier one.

However, there is a way of getting something for nothing here. Aerodynamics. Aerodynamic downforce increases the vertical load on the tires without increasing the work required of the tires. That is why an increase in aerodynamic downforce will always improve the cornering capabilities of a car.

Weight Transfer

One of the keys to driving a car at the limit is controlling the balance of the car. In this case, "balance" describes when the car's weight is equally distributed over all four tires (see the accompanying illustration). When the car is balanced, you are maximizing the tires' traction. The more traction the car has, the more in control the car is and the faster you can drive around the track.

I'm sure you already know that as a car accelerates, the rear end tends to squat down. That's because a percentage of the car's weight has now transferred to the rear

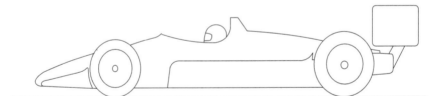

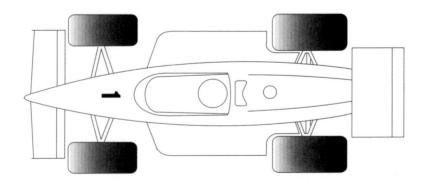

The car, when balanced, has equal traction capacity on each tire.

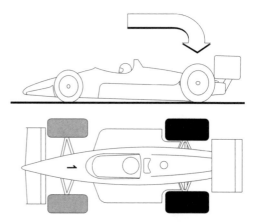

Under acceleration, weight transfers to the rear, increasing rear tire traction.

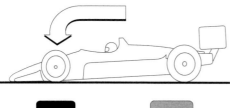

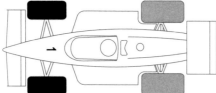

Under braking, weight transfers to the front, increasing front tire traction.

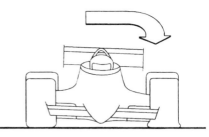

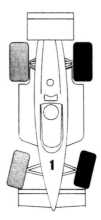

Weight transfers laterally, to the outside, during cornering, increasing the traction of the outside tires and decreasing the inside tires' traction.

45

(see the accompanying illustration). When braking, the car nose-dives—the weight has transferred forward (as illustrated). In a corner, the weight transfers laterally to the outside, causing the car to lean—"body roll" (as shown). The total weight of the car has not changed, just the distribution of the weight.

So, as a car accelerates and weight is transferred to the rear (the back end squatting down), the pressure, or load, on the rear tires' contact patch increases, increasing the rear tire traction. During braking, the opposite happens—the car nose-dives (weight is transferred to the front) and front tire traction increases. While going around a corner, weight transfers to the outside tires, increasing their traction.

However—and this is very important to understand—when the weight transfers onto a pair of tires, increasing their traction, weight is being taken off the other two, decreasing traction. Unfortunately, the overall effect to the car is a decrease in total vehicle traction.

You can, and must, control this weight transfer to your advantage.

Traction Unit Number

Let me explain it this way. If you were to quantify the amount of traction each tire has and give it a corresponding number, that would be what I call the tire's "traction unit number." (This is simply a way of demonstrating the concept—there really is no such thing as a traction unit number.)

Let's take a look at an example (see the accompanying illustration). With a car at rest, or traveling at a constant speed, each tire has, let's say, 10 units of traction—for a total of 40 traction units gripping the car to the road. When you corner, weight is transferred to the outside tires, increasing the vertical load on them, and therefore their traction—giving them 15 units of traction. But, at the same time, weight is transferred away from the inside tires, reducing their vertical load and traction—resulting in only 3 units of traction each. The total traction for the car is now 15+15+3+3=36, which is less than you had before you caused the weight transfer by turning.

As we have already seen in the illustration, vertical load versus traction is not a linear relationship. As load is increased on a tire, traction increases—but not at the same rate as the weight increase. And, as load is decreased from the opposite tire, traction is reduced at a faster rate. The more the weight transfers, the less total traction the car will have.

Balance

Obviously, it is impossible to drive a car without causing some weight transfer. Every single time you brake, corner, or accelerate, weight transfer takes place. However, the less weight transfer that occurs, the more overall traction the car has.

Your goal is to drive in such a way as to keep the weight of the car as equally distributed over all four tires as possible. In other words, balance the car. How? By driving smoothly. Turn the steering wheel as slowly and as little as possible. If you

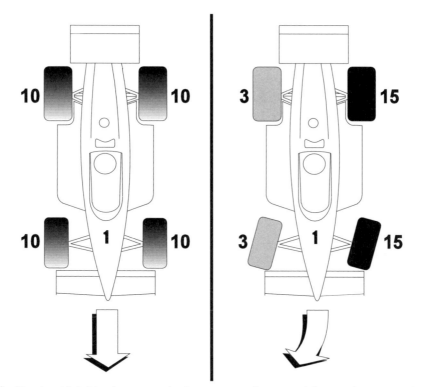

The Traction Unit Number example demonstrates that as weight transfer occurs, the car's overall traction limit is reduced. In other words, the better balanced you keep the car, the more traction it will have, and the faster you can drive through the turns.

jerk the steering wheel into a turn, the car leans or transfers weight a lot; if you turn gently into a corner, the car does not lean as much. Squeeze on and ease off the brakes and gas pedal. Never make a sudden or jerky movement with the controls.

Now you see why it is important to drive smoothly, and how it can affect the balance and overall traction of your car. Again, the greater the weight transfer, the less traction the tires have. And you play the major role in controlling weight transfer and maximizing traction.

Weight transfer and balance also have an effect on your car's handling characteristics, contributing to either understeer, oversteer, or neutral steer, discussed below.

Understeer

Understeer is the term used to describe when the front tires have less traction than the rears, and regardless of your steering corrections, the car continues "plowing" or "pushing" straight ahead to the outside of the turn. Think of it as the car not steering as much as you want, so it is "understeering." Understeer, in effect, increases the radius of a turn.

Accelerating too hard or not smoothly enough through a corner transfers excessive weight to the rear, decreasing traction at the front and causing understeer.

Most drivers' first reaction to understeer is to turn the steering wheel even more. Don't! This increases the problem because the tires were never designed to attack the road at an extreme angle. The tires were meant to face the road with their full profile, not with the sidewall. So, the tires' traction limit has now been further decreased.

To control understeer, decrease the steering input slightly and ease off the throttle gently to transfer weight back to the front. This increases the traction limit of the front tires, as well as reducing speed. Once you have regained front tire traction and controlled the understeer, you can then begin squeezing back on the throttle. Obviously, this easing off and getting back on the throttle will destroy your speed on the following straightaway—and upset the balance of the car. So, make sure you accelerate smoothly the first time.

Oversteer

Oversteer is when the rear tires have less traction than the fronts, the back end begins to slide, and the nose of the car is pointed at the inside of the turn. The car has turned more than you wanted it to, so it has oversteered. This is also called "being loose," "fishtailing," or "hanging the tail out." Its effect is to decrease the radius of a turn.

Turning into a corner with the brakes applied, or lifting off the throttle in a corner ("trailing throttle oversteer") causes the weight to transfer forward, making the rear end lighter, thus reducing rear wheel traction. The result? Oversteer.

Also, if you accelerate too hard in a rear-wheel-drive car, it will produce "power oversteer." What you have done is used up all of the rear tires' traction for acceleration, and not left any for cornering. To control excessive "power oversteer," simply ease off the throttle slightly.

To use oversteer to your advantage, just look and steer where you want to go. This forces you to turn into the slide, or to "opposite lock," thereby increasing the radius of the turn. At the same time, gently and smoothly ease on slightly more throttle to transfer weight to the rear and, thus, increase traction. Whatever you do, avoid any rapid deceleration. This will most likely produce a spin as you decrease the rear wheel traction even more.

Neutral Steer

Neutral steer is the term used to describe when both the front and rear tires lose traction at the same speed or cornering limit, and all four tires are at the same slip angle. Sometimes described as "being in a four-wheel-drift," this is ideally what a driver is striving for when adjusting the handling of the car and trying to balance it.

I love the feeling when I'm controlling the balance of the car with the throttle, driving through a fast, sweeping turn at the limit. If the car begins to oversteer a little, I squeeze on more throttle to transfer a little weight to the rear; if it starts to understeer, I ease off slightly, giving the front a little more grip. When it's done just right, all four tires are slipping the same amount—the car perfectly balanced, neither oversteering or understeering—in a perfect neutral steer attitude through the turn.

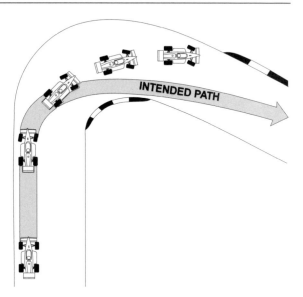

An understeering car does not steer, or turn, as much as you want along the intended path. This is also called "pushing."

In terms of how the car is set up, however, most drivers prefer a little understeer in fast corners as it's a more predictable, safer characteristic; they prefer oversteer in slow corners to assist in pivoting the car around the tight turn.

Taking a Set

"Taking a set in a turn" describes when the car is finished with its weight transfer. It is the point in a turn where all the weight transfer that you are going to cause has occurred. The car is most stable when it has taken a set, and then can be more easily driven to its limit.

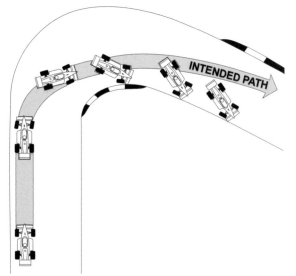

An oversteering car steers, or turns, more than you want, along the intended path. This is also called "being loose."

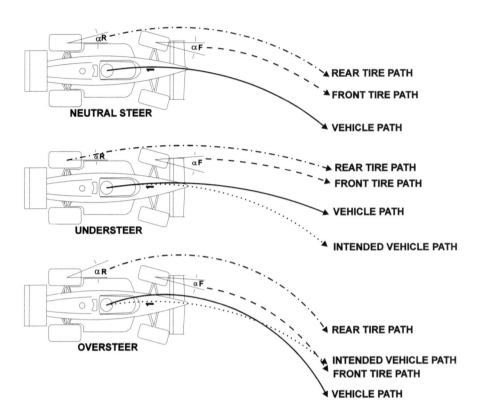

A car whose handling is neutral has equal slip angles front and rear; an understeering car has larger front slip angles than the rear; and an oversteering car has larger rear slip angles than the front.

How quickly the car takes a set in the turn is largely a matter of how the shock absorbers are adjusted, and how you drive. As you turn into a corner, the quicker the weight transfers, the quicker the car takes a set. The sooner the car takes a set, the sooner you can drive the car at its limit, and the faster you will be.

Why? Recall the Traction Unit Number example. As weight transfers, the tire traction available is being reduced. Once all the weight transfer that is going to occur has occurred—and the car has taken a set—you can then work with the traction available and drive at the limit. If you don't make the weight transfer happen quickly enough, you spend most of the corner waiting for the car to take a set, and therefore, waiting a long time before you really know what traction limit you're working with. And if you don't drive smoothly—causing a little weight transfer, then a lot, then less, then more again, all through the same corner—the car will never take a set. It's very difficult to drive at the limit when that limit is constantly changing.

However, before you get any ideas about making the weight transfer occur too quickly, think about the Traction Unit Number example again. If you quickly transfer weight by jerking the steering into a corner, the effect will be more overall weight transferred, and therefore less overall traction.

So, your goal is to make the car take a set in the turn (get to its maximum weight transfer and stay there) as quickly as possible without causing any more weight transfer than necessary. That means smooth, precise, and deliberate actions with the controls.

Dynamic Balance

Getting back to balancing the car, there is also what I call "dynamic balancing" of the car. Very few cars have a perfect 50/50 weight distribution to begin with. Most purpose-built race cars are midengine with a weight distribution around 40 percent front and 60 percent rear, as this is close to ideal for a race car.

Production-based front-wheel-drive cars are usually closer to 65 percent front and 35 percent rear. Only production-looking tube frame race cars (Trans-Am, NASCAR, etc.) are close to 50/50 weight distribution.

Realizing this, a driver must compensate by controlling the weight transfer to balance the car into a neutral handling state (no understeer or oversteer). To do this the driver may have to control the weight transfer so that statically there would be more weight on the front or rear, but dynamically the car is perfectly balanced.

Look at it this way. Let's assume your race car's static or at-rest weight distribution is 40 percent front, 60 percent rear, and it is set up to oversteer at the limit (either on purpose or because you haven't been able to find the right setup). While driving through a 100-miles-per-hour corner, you know you could go quicker if the car oversteered less—if it was neutral handling. To make the car oversteer less, you will have to cause some weight to transfer rearward by squeezing on the throttle. This would change the weight distribution to approximately 35 percent front, 65 percent rear. At speed through a corner, dynamically, this is balanced.

Brake Bias

Keeping this weight transfer in mind, an important factor in braking is how the brake bias is set and/or adjusted. Braking forces are not shared equally by all four wheels. Due to the forward weight transfer under braking, and therefore more front tire traction, most of the braking is handled by the front brakes. The brake forces will be biased toward the front. This is why all vehicles have larger brakes on the front wheels than on the rear.

Actually, you want to adjust the brake bias so that the front wheels will lock up just slightly before the rears. This is a more stable condition, as it gives you more warning of a skid. You will feel it in the steering immediately if the front tires begin to skid. Plus, if the rear tires lock up first, the car will tend to skid sideways.

However, different conditions will require a different ratio, or bias, of front versus rear braking forces. In the rain you will have to adjust the brake bias more to the rear (lower traction limits reduce the amount of weight transferred to the front tires). Some cars also change dramatically as the fuel load lightens during a race. This is where a driver-actuated brake bias adjuster is beneficial.

Practically all purpose-built race cars have an adjusting mechanism for changing the bias. With production-based race cars, you will pretty much have to live with the bias that the factory built into the car. Learn how to "read" and then adjust your race car's brake bias.

Aerodynamics

Aerodynamics come into full effect only at relatively high speeds. Only very sensitive, experienced drivers will feel the effects of aerodynamics at anything under 60 miles per hour. Beyond that, aerodynamics play a big role in the handling of a race car, and therefore, you must learn as much as possible about how to adjust and feel the effects.

In the simplest terms, a race driver is only concerned with two aspects of aerodynamics: drag and lift (both negative and positive lift). Drag is the wind resistance or friction against the body of the vehicle that effectively slows the car down. Lift is the effect the air has on the weighting of the vehicle. Positive lift is the lifting up of the body, which is what airplanes like. Negative lift is the downforce on the body, which is what cars like—or should I say, what drivers like—and helps keep the car in contact with the road.

Aerodynamics can influence the balance of a car and cause it to either understeer or oversteer. This is referred to as the car's "aerodynamic balance." Sometimes a car that understeers at relatively low speeds will begin to oversteer at higher speeds. The low-speed understeer is a result of suspension design and/or set up. But, as the speed increases, bodywork design (including wings if present) begins to affect the situation. A vehicle with more downforce on the front end than on the rear (possibly due to spoilers, wing adjustments, etc.) will have more traction on the front tires as the speed increases, resulting in high-speed oversteer. It is important for you to understand the difference between suspension-induced and aerodynamic-induced handling characteristics.

The balancing of the suspension and aerodynamics is what setting up the car is all about. Many hours are spent developing the handling in the slow corners with suspension adjustments, then changing aerodynamics for the ultimate balance between downforce (front and rear) and drag. Unfortunately, the increase in downforce (resulting in higher cornering speeds) means more drag, resulting in less straight-line speed. The lift (downforce)-to-drag ratio is quite a compromise.

As James Weaver said:

"In roadracing it is very rare that taking wing off results in better lap times. If you look at the data acquisition (the full throttle histogram), you will be surprised at how little you use full throttle—adjusting the aerodynamics makes the most difference. It may be worth reducing wing to help overtaking in race trim; but if you still can't overtake, go back to maximum wing or try late braking. When racing against a car that has less download than you, it may be impossible to get close enough on the straights to outbrake them. However, as the tires degrade, this situation can change dramatically in your favor. I always set my final wing balance on half tanks and with tires that have slightly more miles on them than they would at the end of a stint. The longer the race, the less merit there is in reducing rear wing and it is something I am very wary of."

Another important factor for a driver is how a car in front of another car will affect the trailing car's speed and handling. When the lead car blocks the air, reducing the wind resistance for the second car, the latter car benefits from what is called "drafting" or "slipstreaming." This allows the second car to travel faster, to perhaps pass the leading car or even back off the throttle slightly to conserve fuel.

Another factor, often forgotten, comes into play here as well. With winged and/or ground-effects cars in particular, the car relies on a certain airflow for downforce. When that airflow is blocked by a car in front, the trailing car's cornering ability will be reduced. That is why you will see a car catch up to another quite quickly, and then struggle to get past. When it's running by itself, it is quicker; but when its airflow is reduced, it is no faster than the leading car. As a driver, you must recognize this and not overdrive while following closely behind another car. Perhaps the best strategy is to take a run at the leading car. In other words, hang back a little until you get enough momentum from the draft to pull out quickly and pass on the straightaway.

The first time I drove an Indy car on an oval track, I couldn't believe the effect other cars around me had on the handling of my car. If there was a car in front of me, it took away a lot of the air flowing over my car, causing it to understeer. If there was a car close to my tail, it seemed to make the airflow over the rear wing less effective, causing my car to oversteer. I learned very quickly to make note of the other cars' positions and to predict what they would do to my car. By the way, this doesn't just happen with Indy cars. Any car that relies on aerodynamic downforce for grip will be affected to some extent.

With any car that depends on ground effects for downforce, there's another little trick for you to consider. The faster the car goes, the more downforce, and therefore traction, it has. This can make for an uncomfortable situation when you first begin to drive a ground-effects car. If you reach a point when it feels like the car is at its limit, you may have to drive faster in order to get more downforce. Once you go faster, the car has more grip, and it feels like you're nowhere near the limit—and you're probably not!

Smoothness

As I mentioned earlier—a number of times!—balancing the car is one of the most important and probably most difficult aspects of driving. But, again, balancing is the key. Whenever one or two tires become unweighted due to weight transfer from braking, cornering, or acceleration, they lose traction. So, obviously, you want to cause as little weight transfer as possible. How? By driving smoothly! The less abruptly you apply the brakes, turn the steering wheel, or use the gas pedal, the smoother you will drive, and the more overall traction the car will have. In other words, don't abuse the traction the tires give you.

You've seen how important controlling the weight transfer in the car is, and how to do this with your controls. But you also have to accomplish this with extreme smoothness. If you jerk the steering into a turn, you immediately transfer excessive weight to the outside of the car, reducing your total traction. You will have to wait until the car's weight settles down and is balanced again—taken a set—before being able to corner at the limit and accelerate out of the corner. This wastes time.

SPEED SECRET #12:
Smooth is fast.

The car should be driven absolutely as smoothly as possible all the time. Practice this in your everyday driving. Don't pounce on the gas pedal—squeeze it on and ease off gently. Don't slam on the brakes—squeeze them smoothly and progressively to the threshold braking limit. Don't yank or jerk the steering wheel—smoothly and gently feed in the required steering input that your eyes looking well down the road tell you. Don't bang the shifter into gear—simply place it in gear . . . with finesse.

Keep in mind that each tire has a specific, limited amount of traction. If you exceed that traction limit, the car will begin to skid or slide. The smoother you drive, the easier it will be to stay within those traction limits. A tire achieves a higher traction limit if it has gradually built up to that limit. In other words, if you enter a corner and quickly jerk the

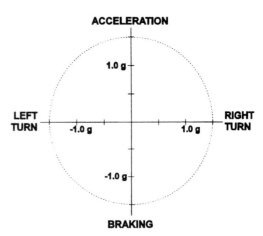

The Traction Circle is a simple X-Y graph that represents the g-forces the car experiences while being driven around the track. In this graph the circle is shown at a theoretical limit of 1.5 g's.

steering wheel into the turn, or jab at the brake pedal when trying to panic stop, you haven't given the tires a chance to build up their traction forces gradually, and they will not be able to hold on; a skid or slide will result.

Think of the tire's traction limit like the force it takes to snap a piece of string. If you gradually and gently pull two ends of the string, it requires a lot of force to break it. However, if you quickly jerk the string apart, it snaps with much less force—just like a tire's traction limit.

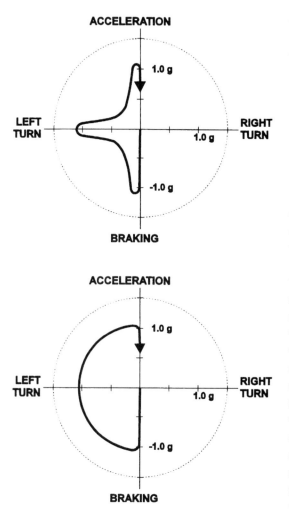

These two Traction Circle graphs represent two ways of driving the same corner. In the graph on top, a lot of the tires' potential is not being used—and time is being wasted. The graph on the bottom shows the correct way to take the corner—the tires' full traction potential is being used.

SPEED SECRET #13: Build up the tire's cornering force slowly.

Everything you do behind the wheel must be done smoothly. When turning into a corner, turn the steering wheel as gently and slowly as possible—this will make the turn smooth! When braking, squeeze the brake pedal, don't jab at it. Believe me, if you squeeze the brakes on, you will stop faster and with more control than if you very quickly jabbed at the pedal. So, always think "squeeze" when applying the brakes—or the throttle. Progressively squeezing the gas pedal down will give more controlled acceleration—even when trying to accelerate in a hurry!

It is better to be smooth than to be fast. Speed will come with practice—practicing smooth driving, that is. Trying to drive fast before learning to be smooth is a mistake. You will never be as fast as if you learn to be smooth first, and let your speed pick up naturally.

Once again, the slower and smoother you move behind the controls, the more in control you will be—and the faster your car will be.

Trail Braking

Trail braking is a term used to describe the technique of continuing braking while turning into a corner. In other words, you brake and turn at the same time. There is a very specific reason for doing this, as explained in the Traction Circle section that follows.

When teaching students in my racing school I used to joke about trail braking being when you spin off the track and through the trees—breaking trail all the way. I sure hope none of them took it seriously!

Traction Circle

The Traction Circle is a simple, graphic way of showing the performance of any driver in any car. Basically, it is an X-Y axis graph (as shown here) produced by a computer data acquisition system (the simplest being the "g-Analyst," which is sold for about $400) of the g-forces that the car experiences during braking, cornering, and acceleration while being driven around a track.

First of all, let's get a grasp of the unit of measure we're using here. One g-force is equal to the force of 1 times the weight of the vehicle; for example, if a 2,000-pound car is cornering at 1.0 g, there is a centrifugal force of 2,000 pounds pushing outward on the car.

Consider that a tire has relatively equal traction limits in each direction—braking, cornering, or acceleration—say, 1.1 g. In other words, the car and tire combination is capable of braking at 1.1 g, cornering at 1.1 g, and accelerating at 1.1g before the tires begin to break away and start to slide. If you exceed the tires' traction limit, they will begin to slide—slowing you down, or, if not controlled, resulting in a spin. On the other hand, if you do not use all the tires' traction available, you will be slow.

These g-forces can be measured and graphed as you drive through the corner. If you use the proper driving technique, the graphed line will somewhat follow a circle—the Traction Circle—telling you that you are using the tire's full potential.

In the transition from one directional force to another, say, from braking to cornering, there are two ways to get from one limit of traction to the other (as shown in the accompanying illustration). You may, upon reaching the end of the braking zone (where you braked at 1.1 g), suddenly lift off the brakes, then turn into the corner (building up to 1.1 g of cornering force). The second option is to ease gradually off the brakes, while at the same time applying more and

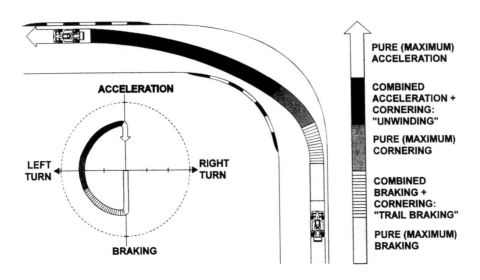

This illustration shows the relationship between what the driver is doing in the corner and the Traction Circle graph.

more steering angle—overlapping some of the braking and cornering. This latter option is trail braking.

In the first scenario the car goes through a short period (perhaps only a fraction of a second) where the tires are not at their limit—they are not being used to their full potential. This wastes time, no matter how short, because the car cannot instantly change from straight-line braking to a curved path. The second scenario, which keeps the tire and car on the outside edge of the Traction Circle graph, is a much faster way of driving a race car. It is also the smoothest way of building traction forces, which, as we know, generates higher cornering speeds.

What you must do—what the Traction Circle is telling you to do (as shown in the illustration)—is to "trail" (gradually ease off) your foot off the brakes as you enter the turn. This is trail braking.

Or, brake at 100 percent of the traction limit (1.1 g) along the straightaway up to the corner, and begin to ease off the brakes as you begin to turn in, trading off some of the braking force for cornering force (90 percent braking, 10 percent cornering; then 75 percent braking, 25 percent cornering; then 50 percent, 50 percent; etc.), until you are cornering at the limit (using 100 percent of the traction for cornering, at 1.1 g). You will start to straighten the line t hrough the corner, "unwining the car" out of the turn early, so the tires have traction capacity for the acceleration phase (90 percent cornering, 10 percent acceleration; 75 percent cornering, 25 percent acceleration; 50 percent cornering, 50 percent acceleration; etc.).

The real key to the Traction Circle is the smooth, progressive overlap of braking, cornering, and acceleration. If you do all your braking prior to turning into the corner, you will waste a lot of the tires' traction capabilities—not to mention being slow. You must drive the limit by balancing and overlapping the braking, cornering, and acceleration forces so you keep the tires at their traction limit at the edge of the Traction Circle. This will lead to the fastest possible lap, and to another type of circle—the winner's circle.

Tires do have a limit to their traction; if you are using 100 percent of the tires' traction for cornering, you can't use even 1 percent for acceleration.

The Traction Circle demonstrates how a tires' traction limit can be used and shared. It shows that if you are using all of the tires' traction for braking, you can't expect to use any for cornering without easing off the brakes; if you are using all the traction for cornering, you can't use any for acceleration until you begin to unwind or release the steering (straighten the wheel); if you are using all the traction for acceleration, you can't still be cornering near the limit.

Here's an easy way to remember this vital relationship between acceleration, braking, and steering: Think of the throttle and brake pedal as being connected to the steering wheel. More steering angle means less brake or throttle pedal pressure. More pedal pressure means less steering angle. Too much steering angle combined with too much pedal pressure puts the tires beyond their traction limit.

Too much steering angle for the amount of braking or acceleration (or vice versa) will cause the car to exceed the traction limit—usually at one end of the car before the other (understeer or oversteer). This can sometimes "trick" you into believing there is a handling problem with the car, when it most likely is your technique—asking either the front or rear tires to do more than they are capable of doing.

When I attended my first racing school, I was taught to do all my braking in a straight line on the approach to a corner, then turn into the corner. Over the next couple of years I gradually learned by trial and error to trail brake. But when I started to race a Trans-Am car a few years later, I had to improve my trail braking—it was the only way to go fast in one of those cars. So, over the next couple of weeks, at night in my street car, I would practice trail braking well into the corners of a deserted industrial park. I didn't have to go fast. I just practiced the technique of trailing off the brakes while turning into the corner, then squeezing back on the throttle while unwinding the steering out of the corner. It really was an effective way of improving my technique.

The Traction Circle demonstrates that the key to driving fast is balancing the pedal application with the steering angle. Learn how to overlap the braking, cornering, and acceleration and you will drive the limit.

Chapter 6

Driving the Limit

As you've seen in the last chapter, to be a winner, you have to use the tires' traction limit. Once you have built up the tires' braking, cornering, or acceleration forces, keep them there—drive the limit. I know it is easy to say, but that's what it takes. Entering the corner, brake at the traction limit—threshold braking. As you reach the point where you begin turning into the corner, start easing off the brakes as you turn the steering wheel. The more you turn the wheel, the more you ease off the brakes (trail braking), until you are completely off the brakes. At this point your vehicle should be at the tires' maximum cornering traction limit. As you start to unwind the steering coming out of the corner, you begin increasing the acceleration until you are at full throttle onto the straight (see the accompanying illustration).

SPEED SECRET #14:
Overlap your braking, cornering, and acceleration forces.

What you want to do is brake at the traction limit, then trade off braking for cornering as you enter the corner; then corner at the traction limit, then trade off cornering for acceleration as you unwind out of the corner; then use full acceleration traction onto the straight. This overlapping of forces must be done with extreme smoothness, resulting in a single, flowing drive through the corner at the limit.

If it's not done smoothly, the car won't be balanced, and the limit will be reduced—possibly at one end of the car sooner than the oth-

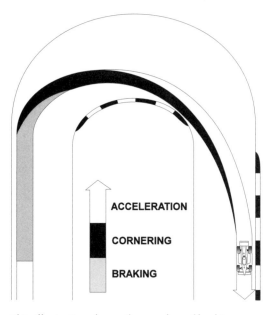

This illustration shows the overlap of braking, cornering, and acceleration.

59

er, causing oversteer or understeer. If done smoothly, though, you can control the oversteer or understeer—at a higher limit or speed—to your advantage to help control the direction or "line" of the car. You do this by what I call "steering the car with your feet"—controlling the balance of the car.

I still remember the first time I experienced steering the car with the throttle. It was at my first racing school course, driving a Formula Ford. As I drove through a fast sweeping turn, I eased off the throttle. The car began to oversteer making it turn a little more into the inside of the corner. I then applied more throttle and it understeered—causing it to point more toward the outside edge of the track. The whole time I kept the steering in the same position. I was thrilled. I could change the direction of the car with my right foot as much as I could with the steering wheel. Of course, what I had learned was the effect weight transfer had on the car when driving at the limit—and how to use that to my advantage. It's still one of the most enjoyable parts of driving for me.

I had a lot of fun with this when teaching high-performance driving and racing techniques at Westwood Motorsport Park in our school BMWs. I would drive through Turn 3 with a couple of students in the car with me, and very quickly turn the steering wheel back and forth, left to right. At the speed we were going—at the limit—the steering would have little to no effect. I would change the direction of the car simply by easing off or on the gas pedal—changing the balance of the car. I think the students learned a lot from that.

PART 2

The Track

Every race track has its own personality. Of course, there are as many shapes and layouts as there are tracks. There are oval tracks (short, long, and superspeedways), permanent roadracing courses, and temporary circuits (constructed on streets or airport runways) of every length and size. But even two tracks with seemingly identical layouts will have a different feel to them.

How well you get to know each track you race on, and how you adapt to them, will play a large role in your success.

In this part of the book, we'll take a detailed look at the race track, and how your knowledge of it will help you drive at the limit.

Chapter 7

Cornering Technique

As a race driver, your goal in each and every corner is really quite simple. Well, simple to state here—maybe not so simple to do. You want to

- Spend as little time in the corner as possible, and
- Get maximum speed out of the corner, by accelerating early, to maximize straightaway speed.

Often, to maximize one of the above means sacrificing the other. In other words, to achieve the best-possible lap times, you may have to compromise corner speed for straightaway speed, or vice versa. It will depend on the specific layout of the track and your car's performance characteristics. The trick is finding the perfect compromise.

The Cornering Compromise

As I discussed in Part 1, becoming a winning race driver requires the ability to drive the race car consistently at the traction limit of the tire/chassis combination (at the limit of the Traction Circle) and the engine. Having said that, virtually anyone can take a car to its limits on the straightaway—using the engine to its limit. It's driving the car at the limit under braking, cornering, and accelerating out of the corner that separates the winners from the also-rans.

Most races, then, are decided where the cars are moving slowest—in the corners. Yet, it is much easier to pass on the straightaways than it is in the corners. So, the faster you are on the straight, the more cars you will pass or gain a time advantage on—and the more races you will win. Therefore, the most important goal for the corners is to drive them in such a way as to maximize your straightaway speed.

The skill comes in determining a speed and path through the corners that take the least amount of time, while ensuring maximum acceleration down the following straightaway. This is where true champions shine.

Winning drivers keep their cars at the Traction Circle limit almost all the time, though the limit does vary depending on track conditions and the state of the car. For example, as I mentioned in the previous section, aerodynamics are constantly changing the limit. The higher the speed the car is traveling, the more aerodynamic downforce there is, thereby developing more cornering force. At the same time, the acceleration capabilities of the engine are reduced as speeds are increased (at low speed in a low gear the engine has lots of relative power to accelerate at or near the traction limits of the tires; at very high speed, the engine does not have the power to accelerate near the traction limit). Therefore, in reality, the Traction Circle changes with speed. The higher the speed, the more the top of the circle flattens out and the sides (the cornering forces) expand. Much of the skill you must develop is in being able to read these changing variables, determine from moment to moment where the performance limit lies, and drive the car as close to it as possible. Much of this comes from experience.

Driving the limit of adhesion—the Traction Circle—through the corners at all times seems like the only thing you have to do to go fast. But how you drive through the corners can vary. How much time you spend at various points on the Traction Circle can vary. And how you determine that and the path or "line" through the corner is critical—it's one of the keys to going fast.

In fact, one of the most important skills to learn is determining the optimum time to spend at the different parts of the Traction Circle limit. While one driver may spend almost all of the time in the pure cornering region, at almost constant speed, another driver may spend more time braking and accelerating, simply by taking a slightly different line through the corner. Both operate the car at its limit all the time; one may be faster through the individual corner, while the other may be faster down the straightaways.

The trick is to determine which line through the corner results in the best overall lap time, not just what is fastest through each individual corner. Considering the corner and the straightaways on either side as a single problem, rather than just worrying about how to get through the corner itself, is the winner's approach.

To determine consistently that optimum line, you have to take into account the track variables, such as the lengths of the straightaways before and after the corner, the angle of the corner, its inside and outside radii, the track's banking (negative or positive), and the track surface's coefficient of friction. And you have to consider the car's variables: its handling characteristics, aerodynamic downforce, acceleration and braking capabilities, and so on. In other words, the optimum solution differs from corner to corner, and from car to car on the same corner.

Before I go any further, let's take a look at a few basics.

Reference Points

To be consistent in your driving, you should use reference points. They are important for your concentration. The less time and concentration you spend determining the exact point where you begin your braking for a corner, for instance, the more you can spend feeling how the car is reacting to your inputs. (More on this in Part 3.)

These reference points can be anything, such as a crack in the pavement, a point on a curbing, a change in pavement, a marking on a wall on the side of the track, a turn worker station, and so on. Notice, though, I do not mention anything that could move during a race, such as a shadow or a turn worker.

James Weaver says: "I like to have reference points on both sides of the track, for when I'm passing. And, it's important to have more points in the rain—higher off the ground if possible—because visibility is such a problem. But don't just rely on your vision. Use your hearing as well. The exhaust note will change as you go past the end of a guard rail, or a gap in the trees, for example. Use these sounds as a 'fail safe' for racing in poor visibility. If the noise goes up unexpectedly, look in the mirrors and check that the wing is still there!"

The three most important reference points are used to help guide you through the corners. They are, in order: the turn-in point, apex, and exit point (see the accompanying illustration). Each point is discussed in detail below, but the ultimate goal is to combine all three into a smooth, fluid line through a corner by connecting the dots first visually, and then physically.

The turn-in is probably the most important part of a corner, as this determines how you drive the rest of the corner—where and how fast you apex and exit. As the name suggests, this is the part of a track where you do your initial turning of the steering wheel into the corner. The turn-in point is determined somewhat by where you want to apex the corner.

The apex of a corner is the point, or area, where the inside wheels run closest to the inside of the road. The apex can also be thought of as the area of a turn where you are no longer driving into the corner, but are now driving out. It is sometimes called the "clipping point" as this is where your inside wheels clip past the inside of the roadway.

The location of the apex is determined by where and how you entered the turn, and it will affect how you exit it. The ideal apex for a corner can be either early in the turn, in the middle of it, or late in the turn.

Determining whether you had the correct apex is very simple. If you come out of the corner having to turn more to keep from running off the road, then your apex was too early. If you chose too late an

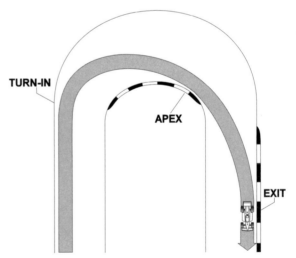

A typical 180-degree hairpin turn showing the three most important reference points: the turn-in, apex, and exit.

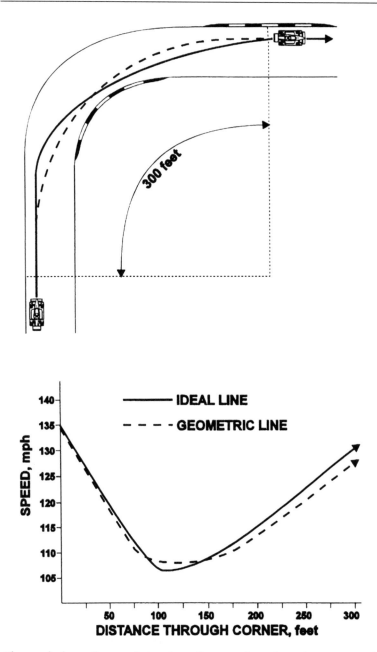

300 feet

SPEED, mph

IDEAL LINE

GEOMETRIC LINE

DISTANCE THROUGH CORNER, feet

The graph shows the speed at various distances throughout the corresponding corner. The dotted geometric line is faster through the actual corner; the solid Ideal Line is a little slower in the early part of the corner, but allows earlier acceleration, resulting in a much quicker exit speed. The extra speed at the exit will continue—and multiply— all the way down the following straightaway.

apex, the car will not be using all the road on the exit—it will still be too close to the inside of the corner.

In most corners, if you are doing anything with the steering wheel other than unwinding it after the apex of the corner, you are probably on the wrong line. Most likely, you have turned in and apexed too early. You shouldn't be turning the steering wheel tighter once past the apex.

When you hit the apex perfectly, the car will naturally want to follow a path out to the exit point—the point where your car runs closest to the outside edge of the track. In fact, to exit the corner properly you must use up all the track. Allow the car to come out wide to the edge of the road. This allows the car to balance its weight smoothly and gently and achieve maximum acceleration. It allows you to "unwind" the car.

I know when I've hit the perfect apex. It's when I'm able to stay just barely on the track at the exit, while accelerating as early and hard as possible. If I have to ease up slightly on the throttle to stay on the track, then I apexed too early. If I wasn't able to unwind the steering after the apex, I apexed too early. But, if I still have room left on the exit, then I apexed too late.

The Ideal Line

You can adjust the amount of time spent on each part of the Traction Circle by taking different lines through a corner. The adjacent illustration shows two possibilities. The dotted line shows the "geometric line," that is, a constant radius through the corner. This is the fastest way through that particular corner. The solid line shows an altered line in which the driver has started to turn later. The line is tighter than the geometric line at the beginning, but exits in a wider, expanding radius further down the following straightaway.

The second line, the solid line, is called the "Ideal Line," and will generally result in an overall faster lap time. Why?

As I said earlier, you are not just dealing with one particular corner, but rather a series of corners connected by straightaways. Considering this, plus the fact that you will spend more time accelerating on a race track than you will just cornering, superior exit speed is far more important than cornering speed.

It doesn't matter how fast you go through the corner—if everyone passes you on the straight, you won't win a race. Drive the corner in such a way as to maximize your straightaway speed.

Never forget that the driver who accelerates first out of a corner will arrive first at the other end of the straight, and most often the finish line.

SPEED SECRET #15:
Races are won on the straightaway, not in the corners.

SPEED SECRET #16:
It is better to go into a corner slow and come out fast, rather than vice versa.

The driver following the geometric line in the illustration spends almost all the time at the limit in the "cornering only" region of the Traction Circle, keeping the speed nearly constant throughout the corner. Remember what the Traction Circle told us: you cannot begin to accelerate if you are using all the traction for cornering. Therefore, the geometric line does not allow you to accelerate until you've reached the very end of the corner and begun to straighten out the steering.

The Ideal Line, on the other hand, with its tighter radius at the beginning of the corner forces you to enter slightly slower, but the gentler, expanding radius through the remainder of the corner allows increasingly more acceleration, and therefore higher exit speed. This higher exit speed stays with you all the way down the following straightaway (and even multiplies its effect), more than making up for the slower entrance speed.

Driving the Ideal Line, you will spend less time at maximum cornering on the Traction Circle. You will spend more time at the braking and acceleration limit, however.

Determining how much to alter the path from the geometric line is one of the more complex problems facing a race driver. Altering it too much—turning in too late and probably apexing too late—means the initial part of the corner must be taken so slowly that the time lost there cannot be recouped fully in the following straightaway. It will result in a slower overall lap time. Not alter-

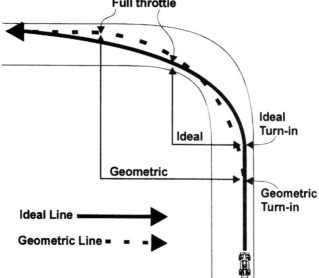

The effective length of any corner is really from the turn-in to the point where you can get back to full throttle. This illustration demonstrates how much less time you spend cornering by using a late apex. Also note how much more straightaway there is prior to the turn-in point for braking—or, how much longer the straightaway is for maximum speed—with the later turn-in.

ing the line enough—turning in and apexing too early—results in a slow exit and straightaway speed.

As I said, there is no single Ideal Line for all cars or corners. The same car driven through different corners requires different lines. Even for the same corner, different cars will require different lines.

The difference may be subtle—perhaps a couple of inches either way; but it makes all the difference in the world—between being a winner or being just a midpack driver.

SPEED SECRET #17:
The more time you spend with the front wheels pointed straight ahead—or near straight—and the throttle to the floor, the faster you will be.

In general, the shorter and tighter the corner, and the longer the following straightaways on either side, the more the line should be altered from the geometric line: in other words, a later turn-in and apex. Similarly, the greater the acceleration capabilities of the car, the later the turn-in and apex.

Many drivers seem to fall into the habit of driving all corners the same. They fail to adjust their driving appropriately for the different conditions—corners or cars—even though they may drive the car at its traction limit. This may explain why some drivers can be very fast in one type of car or at one track, and yet may struggle when they get into another car or drive another track. A true champion driver can quickly alter his line to suit the track and car—and of course, always drive the limit.

James Weaver says: "As a race progresses, and more and more rubber is put down on the track surface, grip can change through a corner and make it impossible to take the ideal line smoothly. In this situation, drive where the grip is, and do whatever is fastest. In a long race, I will always try different lines if necessary. As the 'marbles' build up on the outside of the corners, this normally means turning in slightly earlier and 'flatter,' and hanging onto the apex slightly longer. To make this work, you may need to brake later and diagonally, so that your effective turn-in point is now in the middle of the road, not at the edge."

Control Phases

Breaking the cornering technique down further, there are six activities or phases you go through with your feet on the throttle or brakes in a corner (see the accompanying illustration): braking, trail braking, transition, balanced throttle, progressive throttle, and maximum acceleration. The length and timing of each of these phases will vary depending on the car you're driving and the type and shape of corner. And when you add the turn-in, apex, and exit reference points to the equation, you have the formula for a successfully completed corner.

Taking a closer look at the braking phase, think of the brakes as a waste of

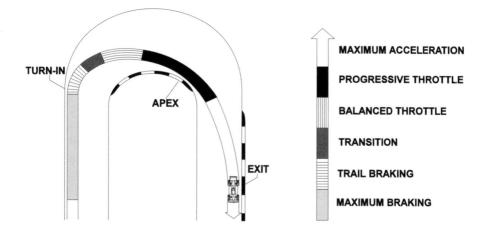

The control phases of a corner.

time. Brakes are merely for adjusting speed—not for gaining much. So, if you are looking to improve more than 1/10th of a second on an average roadracing circuit, don't just look at the brakes. Don't think that by braking later you'll gain a great advantage. You're going to make up more time with the throttle on, not off.

Racers are always talking about brake reference points. They're always comparing and bragging about how late they begin braking for a corner. But the important reference point is not where you start braking, but actually where you end maximum braking. Only use brake reference points as backup.

Instead, when you begin braking for a corner, focus on the turn-in point to visualize and judge how much braking is necessary to slow the car to the proper speed for entering the turn. Your speed at the start of braking may be different due to how well you entered the straight, so that reference point will constantly need slight adjustment. You need to analyze and sense the speed, and adapt your braking zone to be at the correct speed at the turn-in reference point so you enter the corner at the ideal speed.

SPEED SECRET #18:
The less time spent braking, the faster you'll be.

I always wondered why I often couldn't remember where I started braking for a corner—where my braking point was. This was until I realized that I concentrated more on where I needed to have my maximum braking completed—the turn-in point—and the speed I wanted to slow to, instead of the start-of-braking point. Every driver has their weak and strong points. One of my strong points has always been in the braking area, which I attribute to my concentration on this "end-of-braking" point.

The most controversial control phase is definitely trail braking. Some "experts" say you should never trail brake—complete all your braking and be back on the gas by the time you reach the turn-in point. Others say you should trail brake at every corner on every track. Of course the truth really lies somewhere in between. In some corners in some cars you need to trail brake a lot, and in others you need to do very little to none. It varies depending on the corner and the car you're driving. Your job is to determine what works best.

How do you determine how much to trail brake in each corner (and car)? Begin by asking yourself, Does the car turn in to the corner well? If not, try trail braking a little more—gradually easing (trailing) your foot off the brakes as you turn in. Or, Does the car feel unstable or unbalanced going through the turn? If so, try coming off the brakes and getting back on the throttle just as you turn in. In this case, there may not be a trail braking phase at all.

The transition from braking to acceleration is one area of your technique that may adversely affect the balance of the car most. You should be able release the brakes and begin application of the throttle without feeling the transition whatsoever—and as quickly as possible. It should be immediate, as fast as you can possibly move your foot from the brake pedal to the throttle.

Practice this when driving your street car. You should never be able to feel the point where you ease off the brake pedal and begin to squeeze on the throttle.

A correctly executed transition from braking to acceleration is paramount. It must be done with perfect smoothness. That's one reason why one driver can make a car turn into the corner at a slightly higher speed than another driver. Just because you cannot make your car turn into the corner at a specific speed does not mean Michael Schumacher or Al Unser, Jr., couldn't. Maybe you are not using the correct technique—not being smooth enough, turning the steering too quickly, unbalancing the car, and so on. Again, how you lift your foot off the brakes is absolutely critical. It has to be eased off the pedal—quickly—so as not to upset the balance of the car. Then, you have to transition over to the throttle so smoothly that you never actually feel the exact point where you have come off the brakes and where you start to apply acceleration.

Remember the Traction Circle. The relationship between steering position and throttle position is interactive. Steering input must be reduced ("unwound") in order to apply acceleration. Since a tire has a limited amount of traction, you cannot use all of it to turn the car and expect it to accelerate at the same time. You have to trade off steering input as you begin to accelerate, otherwise you "pinch" the car into the inside of the corner on the exit, often causing the car to spin—and always scrubbing off speed.

And remember, given relatively equal cars, the driver who begins accelerating earliest and hardest will be the fastest on the straightaway. I think that tells you everything you need to know about the progressive throttle and maximum acceleration phases.

Prioritizing Corners

Some corners on a race track are more important than others. Fast lap times, and winning races, come from knowing where to go fast and where to go (relatively) slow. When learning any track, concentrate on learning the most important corners first.

When you analyze any track, you will find that there are only three types of corners:

- One that leads onto a straightaway
- One that comes at the end of a straightaway, and
- One that connects two other corners.

Some people believe the most-important corner, in terms of lap speed, is one that leads onto a straightaway; the next most-important is one that comes at the end of a straight with very little straight after; and the least-important is a corner between corners. This way of prioritizing corners was really made popular by Alan Johnson in his 1971 book, *Driving in Competition*.

The reasoning here is since it's easier to pass on the straightaway, and on most race tracks you spend more time accelerating than you do cornering, it's most important to maximize your straightaway speed—to take advantage of all that time spent accelerating. The corner that leads onto a straight will determine your straightaway speed. If you don't begin accelerating early, you will be slow on the straight.

This way of analyzing and prioritizing types of corners is not a bad place to start. But if you want to win, there is more to it than this.

SPEED SECRET #19:
Before you can win, you have to learn where to go fast.

Based on the type and speed of corners and lengths of straightaways, this map prioritizes the corners at Road Atlanta. Prioritizing corners at each track you race tells you which ones you should concentrate on first, and most, regarding your driving and the car's setup.

There is far more to gain or lose in a track's fast turns than in the slow turns. In fast corners, since your car has less acceleration capabilities, it is much more difficult to make up for the loss of even 1 mile per hour than it is in slow turns.

Let's look at an example, comparing a slow turn—one usually taken at around 50 miles per hour—and a fast turn taken at around 120 miles per hour. If you make an error and lose 5 miles per hour in the slow turn, it is relatively easy for your car to accelerate from 45 to 50 miles per hour. But, your car will not accelerate from 115 to 120 miles per hour as quickly.

Another reason the fastest corners are the most important is that many drivers are intimidated by them. Plus, in most cases, the slow corners are easier to learn. The sooner you perfect the fast corners, the sooner you will have an advantage over your competition.

So, the most important corner is the fastest corner that leads onto a straightaway. The second most important is the next-fastest that leads onto a straight, and so on down to the slowest corner that leads onto a straight.

Your next priority is the corners at the end of straightaways, which do not have usable straights after them. Again, start with the fastest corners and work on down to the slowest.

Finally, concentrate on your speed through the corners that link other corners together.

Analyze where your car works best, as it will handle better in some types of corners than in others. It's a compromise deciding whether to change the car to suit a more important corner. Again, the priority should be to work at making the car handle well for the fastest corners leading onto straightaways.

SPEED SECRET #20:
The most important corner is the fastest one leading onto a straightaway.

Different Corners—Different Lines

The Ideal Line in a corner that leads onto a straightaway (see the adjacent illustration) is one with a late apex, approximately two-thirds of the way through the corner. This allows you to accelerate very early in the corner.

In any turn leading onto a straight it is best to brake early, get the car well balanced as you turn-in, and then accelerate hard onto the straight.

When a straight leads into a corner that is not followed by a usable straight— one that is long enough to allow passing or being passed (see the adjacent illustration)—an early apex is used. Why? Well, since there is not a lot to be gained on the exit of the turn, you want to maximize the benefit of your entrance-straight speed. In other words, sacrifice the corner's exit speed to maintain the straightaway speed for as long as possible. To do this, brake as late as possible, take an early

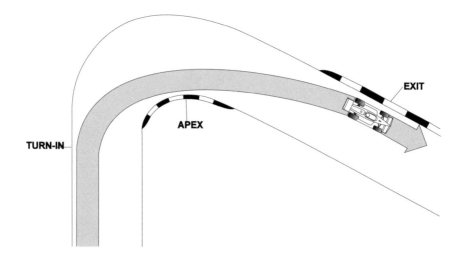

To drive a corner that leads onto a straightaway, your priority is the exit speed onto the following straightaway. This means a relatively late turn-in and apex (at least two-thirds of the way through the turn), early acceleration, and using all the track surface at the exit. Given relatively equal cars, the driver who begins accelerating first will be fastest on the straightaway.

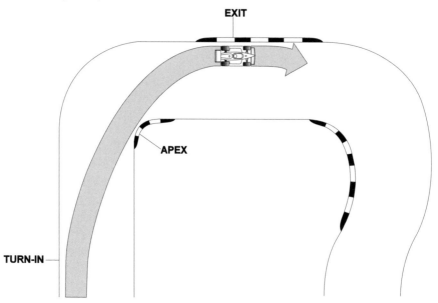

Your goal in a corner at the end of a straightaway that does not lead onto another straightaway is to make the preceding straight as long as possible by braking into the turn. Once you are past the apex and you have slowed down the car enough, then tighten the radius and head toward the exit point.

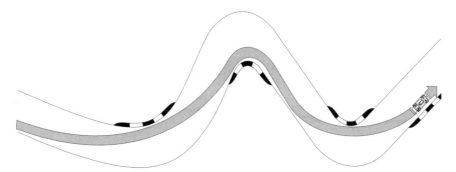

When dealing with a corner that links two other corners, your main concern is your exit speed onto the ensuing straight. That often means sacrificing the line through the "linking" turn to maximize speed through the previous and following corners.

apex, continue braking into the turn, and position the car for whatever comes after this corner.

Now I'm sure you're saying, "Well, lots of corners at the end of a straight also lead onto a straight." You're right. When this is the case, drive them like a corner leading onto a straight, taking a late apex. Again, straightaway speed is of utmost importance. A corner leading onto a straightaway always has priority over one at the end of a straight.

That is why you won't experience many of these types of corners. However, they do exist, and it's important to recognize them and know how to deal with them when you do come across them.

The last type of corner is the compound curve—where two or more turns are linked together, such as "S" bends (see the accompanying illustration). The rule here is to get set up for the last curve that leads onto a straightaway. Drive this last corner as you would any corner leading onto a straight—with a late apex. The first curves in the series are unimportant and must be used to get set up for the last one. Try to get into a smooth gentle rhythm in this series of turns.

Any time you have a succession of corners, your main concern should be the last turn. Again, concentrate on carrying good speed out onto the straightaway. Drive the corners in such a way as to maximize your performance through the final corner leading to the straight.

Oval Track Technique

It used to be that a book like this only talked about driving road courses. But more and more forms of racing in North America are including oval track races as part of their series. I'm not going to go into great detail about strategies and so on, but let's take a look at some basic techniques and tips specific to driving on an oval.

First, car setup. Generally, the car should be set up to understeer slightly—not oversteer. It's next to impossible to control an oversteering (loose) car on an oval, due to the consistently high speeds. You may be able to control it for a couple of laps, but eventually it will catch up with you, sending you spinning into the wall. On an oval, you want to base your car's setup around what the front end is doing, not the rear, as you would on a road course.

Driving an oval—particularly superspeedways—requires more smoothness, finesse, and precision than roadracing. Concentrate on turning the steering more gently and smoothly—arcing into the turn. However, getting the car to take a set in the turns is critical on an oval, so don't turn too slowly.

The Ideal Line on an oval varies depending on the turn's banking, its shape, and the handling of your car. You need to "feel" your way through the corners more so than on a road course; you need to let the car run where it needs to go. Everything I said earlier about the cornering compromise, reference points, and control phases applies to oval tracks as well. And just like on a road course, your straightaway speed is dictated by how well you exit the corners.

In fact, momentum is everything on an oval. The smallest error or lift of the throttle will have a tremendous effect on your lap speed. Don't over-slow the car entering the turn. Try easing off the brakes just slightly sooner than you think possible and let the car run—carry its momentum.

On an oval—as you would on a road course—you want to wait as long as possible before getting off the throttle and beginning to brake. This means you are going to brake into the turns, even more than you would on a road course. But gently. Remember the Traction Circle. You can't brake as hard while turning as you could in a straight line. You have to ease the brakes on.

Looking far ahead is especially important on an oval. When driving an oval, I try to look as far ahead as I can, then just think about getting there as quickly as possible. This may sound obvious, but it helps. Often, a driver's natural reaction is to look at the wall or the point you're just about to get to. That's not enough. You won't drive a smooth, flowing line if you don't look far ahead. And looking well ahead, and concentrating on getting to where I'm looking, seems to really help me.

Traffic on an oval is an entirely different experience than in roadracing. On the smaller ovals especially (one mile or less), you are constantly dealing with other cars—either passing or being passed. Using your mirrors and peripheral vision is particularly important in oval racing.

Turbulence from other cars is a tricky factor on ovals. Passing another car may be difficult, as the closer you get the less downforce you will have (the leading car blocking the airflow to your car), slowing your speed. You have to ease off and try going into a corner a little slower, then accelerate earlier to get a good run out of the corner and slipstream past on the straight.

A car closely following you on superspeedways can affect the handling of your car. When a car gets close to your rear wing or tail, the airflow over the rear is disturbed, decreasing downforce and causing the car to oversteer.

Before my first Indy race on an oval, I was given some very good advice: "If the car doesn't feel right on an oval, don't force it." On a road course you can overcome a bad-handling car somewhat by changing your technique slightly. This is very difficult—and dangerous—on an oval. This means that the car's setup is more critical on an oval. Also, if it feels as though there is a mechanical problem with the car, come into the pits and have it checked. The result of a mechanical breakage on an oval is serious.

Cornering Speed

Don't you wish there was a magic formula to figure out the optimum speed for each car/corner combination? Well, in fact there is. The tire companies, Formula One, and some Indy car teams use a sophisticated computer simulation program to determine tire compounding and construction and chassis setups based on cornering speed. After plugging in hundreds of variables about the car and track, the computer will determine the exact theoretical speed at which the car will be at the limit. What's interesting is that a good driver can usually go faster than the computer says is possible. So, it's still up to us to figure out what speed we can drive each particular turn of the track.

However, using a very simple mathematical formula, and knowing some basic information (radius of the turn and coefficient of friction between the tire and the track surface; and assuming it's an unbanked track), you can calculate the approximate theoretical maximum cornering speed through a turn. Obviously, this is of little "real world" value—how could you ever drive through a corner while ac-

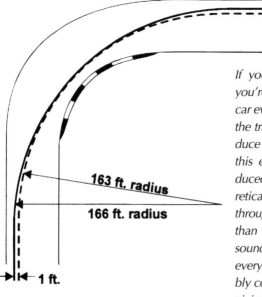

163 ft. radius

166 ft. radius

1 ft.

If you don't use all the track width, you're giving up speed. By keeping the car even one foot away from the edge of the track at the turn-in and exit, you reduce the corner's radius significantly. In this example, the corner radius is reduced by three feet, meaning the theoretical maximum speed you can drive through the corner is reduced by more than 1/2 mile per hour. That may not sound like much, but if you do that at every corner on the track, it will probably cost you .3 or .4 of a second—that's giving time away.

curately monitoring your speed? What this mathematical exercise can do, though, is bring up a very important point.

Let's look at a 90-degree right-hander that has a theoretical maximum cornering speed of 80 miles per hour. By not using all the track surface—entering the corner 1 foot away from the edge of the track, and exiting 1 foot away—you have reduced the radius of the turn to the point where the theoretical maximum speed is now slower—just over 79 miles per hour. Even though that's only a little more than a 1 percent decrease in speed, 1 percent of a 1-minute lap time is more than half a second. And that's a lot of time to waste by not using all the road!

What this demonstrates is the extreme importance of using every little bit of track surface available, and just how critical the Ideal Line is to your cornering speed.

Combined with a precise line through a corner, you must develop a very delicate sense of traction and sense of speed, as this is what ultimately determines your cornering speed. But remember: Increasing your radius through a corner effectively increases the speed you can carry, and vice versa. We'll look at this again in Part 3.

Winning Priorities

Looking at what separates the winners from the losers gives us a guideline as to how to approach learning to drive at the limit:

What separates the winning novice racers from the losing novices? The line—choosing the Ideal Line on a consistent basis.

What separates the winning club racers from the losing club racers? The acceleration phase of the corner—how early and hard they get on the power.

What separates the winning pro racers from the losing pros? Corner entry speed—how quickly they can make the car enter the turn without delaying the acceleration phase.

What separates the greats from the rest? Midcorner speed—how much speed they carry through the middle of turn.

Now, before you get any ideas about trying to carry blazing speed through the middle of every corner, realize that the greats became great only after perfecting the line, the acceleration phase, and the corner entry speed. What this demonstrates is a priority list of how to drive at the limit and become a great race driver.

Chapter 8

The Track

B efore you can consistently drive at the limit, you need to know the track well. That doesn't just mean knowing which direction each corner goes—although that's part of it. It really involves knowing every last detail about the track. With some tracks this takes longer than with others.

When "reading" the track, think about the track surface (asphalt/concrete types, bumps, curbs, etc.), turn radius (decreasing, increasing, constant, tight, large, etc.), road camber (banking—positive, negative, even), elevation changes (uphill, downhill, hillcrests), and the length of the straightaways (short, long).

On a track that is new to you, drive all corners with a very late apex at first. This will allow you a little extra room on the exit if you find the turn is slightly tighter than you thought. Then, with each lap, move the apex earlier and earlier in the turn until you are beginning to run out of track on the exit. Then go back to where you could accelerate out of the corner and still stay on the track. That's the ideal apex.

The banking of a turn may be one of the most critical factors you need to consider. Earlier, I said the radius of a turn determines your speed through it. Well, in fact, the radius of the turn may not be as important as its banking in terms of cornering speed.

When driving a positive banked corner, try to get into the banking as soon as possible and stay in it as long as possible. This probably means turning in a little earlier than would be normal if it were not banked. Many drivers underestimate the additional traction resulting from a banked corner. Use the banking to your advantage.

With off-camber (negative banking) corners, set up so that you are in the off-camber section for as short a time as possible. Also, the banking may vary from the top of the track to the bottom, so look at the track closely. You might not notice the banking when driving through a corner. That is why it is important to walk a track, making note of the detail changes.

Watch for the uphill and downhill sections of the track. They will have a great effect on the traction limit of the car. You want to use these elevation changes to your advantage and minimize their disadvantages. Just remember, a car going uphill has better traction than one going downhill, as the forward motion of the car tends to push it into the track surface, increasing the vertical load on all four tires. Your goal is to do as much braking, turning, and accelerating as possible on the uphill sections, and as little as possible on the downhill portions.

Make note of pavement changes, especially in the middle of a corner. You may want to alter your line to take advantage—or lessen the disadvantage—of where there is maximum grip. You want to make most of your turn on the grippiest pavement and then run straight on the less grippy pavement.

After cars have run on a track for any length of time, an accumulation of bits of rubber from the tires, stones, and dust will end up just outside of the Ideal Line. These are called "the marbles," because of how slippery they feel when you drive on them. Try to stay out of this area. If, because you moved off-line to let another car pass, you had to drive through the marbles, your tires will pick up some of these bits of rubber and stones and they will not have much grip when you get to the next corner. Be careful. Usually, they will clean off once you've driven through one or two more turns.

Walking the Track

Walking the track will help you learn to drive it quickly. However, many drivers make the mistake of turning it into a major social event, walking with a large group of friends. You will learn and remember the track a lot better if you walk it by yourself, or possibly with one other driver who will give you a few tips or suggestions. Remember also to walk the track exactly in line with where you are going to see it from—the driver's seat. Even squat down to see elevation and asphalt changes and how the track looks from the height of your driving position.

Once you've driven a number of tracks, it gets easier. Every time you go to a new track, a corner will remind you of one from another track. You then take that information and apply it to the new corner. This is where experience really pays off.

Having walked tracks for years, I now never walk one until after I've driven it at least for one session. Often, I found that if I walked a track before having a little real experience, I would get false thoughts and ideas of how to drive it. What may have looked like a third-gear corner while walking the track may really have been a fourth-gear corner. Then, before I could start to learn the track properly, I first had to "unlearn" the false thoughts and ideas.

So what I do now is first study a map of the track just to get the direction clear in my head. Then I explore it during the first practice session, trying different gears in the various corners and concentrating on the most important turns first. Then, at the end of the day, I walk it to really work out the details, checking my thoughts and ideas regarding track surfaces, banking, reference points, areas where it is safe to run off the track, and so on. And then, if possible, I try to do a number of laps in a street car at very low speed. This helps program every last detail into my head.

Learning the Track

When learning a new track, you face two hurdles before you will be able to drive consistently at the limit:

- Discovering and perfecting the Ideal Line, and
- Driving the car at its traction limit on that Ideal Line.

It is usually easiest to focus on learning a new track in that order: the line first, and then driving it at the limit. When first learning the Ideal Line around a track, it is important to use all the track surface, even if that means forcing the car toward the edge of the track. At the entrance to the turn—at the turn-in point—it is easy to drive the car to within inches of the edge of the track. At the apex, you need to be right against the inside edge or curb. And, at the exit, drive the car to within a couple of inches of the edge—even use the curb or drop a wheel over the edge to see what it feels like (remember, you're driving relatively slowly at this point).

I hear a lot of drivers talk about how they can always find the right line for a corner simply by following the path of dark black tire marks—"the groove" they call it. They're wrong. The dark black tire marks are a result of drivers trying to tighten their line or make a correction: either feeding in massive amounts of steering—causing understeer—or controlling the back end of the car from a slide—oversteer. When walking a track, follow the path of a really dark tire mark. It usually ends up going off the track to the outside, or spinning back across to the inside. The Ideal Line, or "groove," is usually just inside of the really dark black line through a turn. So, yes, you can use the dark black tire marks as a guide, but don't follow them.

As your speed increases, the car will naturally flow or run out to the edge of the track—if you are driving the Ideal Line and if you don't hold the car in tight (pinching it). Remember to let the car run free at the exit. If you hold the car in at the exit, you have greatly increased your chances of spinning, and you are scrubbing off speed—or you can't get on the power as early as necessary.

When you first learn a track it's important to force yourself to use every inch of it; make it a habit, a programmed, subconscious act. Before moving on to the second part of learning a new track—driving at the limit—the Ideal Line must be a habit. Driving the line must be a subconscious act. It is very difficult to concentrate on two things at once—the line and the amount of traction you have (traction sensing) to determine whether you are at the limit or if you can carry more speed or accelerate sooner/harder.

After the Ideal Line becomes a habit—a subconscious act or program—you can begin to work on driving at the limit. The key here is sensing the amount of traction you have. With each lap, begin accelerating a little earlier and harder out of each corner (actually, remember the corner priorities—fastest corner leading onto a straight, etc.), sensing the amount of traction available. Keep accelerating earlier until you either begin to run out of track or the car begins to understeer or oversteer excessively.

Remember, the car must be sliding (understeering, oversteering, or neutral steering) somewhat, otherwise you're not driving at the limit. Once you feel you're getting close to the limit under acceleration (on the Ideal Line), then begin to work on your corner entry speed. Working on the fastest corners first on down to the slowest, carry a little more speed into the turn each lap, until you can't make the car turn in toward the apex the way you would like—until it begins to understeer or oversteer excessively in the first one-third to one-half of the corner—or it hurts your ability to get back on the power as early as you could before.

Don't forget that when working on the acceleration or corner entry phase, just because you sense you've reached the limit, that doesn't mean you can't go faster still. It may be that the technique you are using now results in reaching the limit, but by changing that technique slightly you may be able to accelerate earlier or carry more speed into the corner—raise that limit. For example, you sense the car is beginning to oversteer too much under power on the exit of the corner. You've reached the limit—with the way you are applying the throttle now. But if you apply the throttle a little smoother, more progressively, the car may stay more balanced and not oversteer as much. Another example: You carry more and more speed into a corner until it begins to understeer as you initiate the turn. You've reached the limit with the technique you're using now. However, if you used a little more braking while you turned (keeping the front tires more heavily loaded), or turned the steering wheel more "crisply," perhaps it wouldn't understeer at all.

The point is not to believe you've reached the ultimate limit just because the car slid a little one time. Once you're used to accelerating that early or carrying that much speed into a corner, take a number of laps to see if you can't make the car do what you want by altering your technique slightly.

Corner entry speed and exit acceleration are related. If your corner entry speed is too low you tend to try to make up for that by accelerating very hard. The hard acceleration may exceed the rear tires' traction limit, causing oversteer. If your corner entry speed was a little higher, you wouldn't accelerate so hard and wouldn't notice any oversteer.

Of course, if your corner entry speed is too high, it may result in getting on the power late. This is going to hurt your straightaway speed. To recap the strategy for learning a new track:

• The line: At a slightly slower speed (difficult to do in a race weekend practice session with other cars around), drive the Ideal Line until it becomes habit—a subconscious, programmed act.

• Corner exit acceleration: Working from the fastest corner leading onto a straight down to the slowest, begin accelerating earlier and earlier until you sense the traction limit.

• Corner entry speed: Working from the fastest corner to the slowest corner, gradually carry more and more speed into the turn until you sense the traction limit.

• Evaluate and alter technique if required: Try accelerating more progressively or abruptly, trail braking more or less, turning in more crisply or more gently, a slightly different line—whatever it takes to accelerate earlier and carry more speed into the corners.

Chapter 9

Making Errors

Every race driver makes errors. Being able to recognize and then analyze your errors is important. Until you can do that, you cannot even begin to correct them and improve. I'm not suggesting that you dwell on them. However, so you might be able to recognize some of your errors a little earlier, here's a look at a few of the most common ones.

I know this part really well—I've made enough errors myself! In fact, I think one of the things that separates a good driver from a not-so-good driver is that the good driver has made more errors—and learned from them. I know that I can consistently push closer to the limit than some less-experienced drivers, simply because I've gone beyond the limit enough to know how to survive—I know how to recover from a mistake. That only comes with experience.

Probably the most common error for race drivers of all levels is turning into the corner too early—prior to reaching the ideal turn-in point (see the accompanying illustration). Ultimately, this will result in an early apex and running out of track on the exit. To avoid running off the track, you will have to ease off the throttle to tighten up the corner and regain the Ideal Line. Obviously, this is going to hurt your straightaway speed. The trick to correcting this error is to use an easy-to-identify turn-in point, know exactly where the apex and exit points are, and be able to see them in your head before getting there.

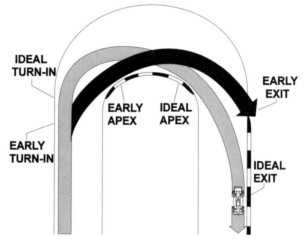

Here's an example of what happens when you turn in too early for a corner. You end up with an early apex and then run out of track at the exit. Of course, if you realize you turned in and apexed early, you can try to slow down gently (remember what happens if you lift off the throttle suddenly while turning) and tighten your radius to get back on line.

Often, turning in too soon is caused by braking too early. A driver brakes too early, slows the car down to the desired entry speed 10 feet before the turn-in point, and then turns. Obviously, the easiest way to cure this problem is simply to brake a little later.

Another common error, with the same result, is turning into the corner too quickly or sharply. What happens is you turn in at the correct point, but turn so sharply that it results in an early apex again. Correct this by knowing in your head where the apex and exit points are before you begin to turn-in. Also you must learn to turn the steering wheel slower.

As I mentioned earlier, using all the road on the exit is important. However, just driving to the edge for the sake of driving the Ideal Line without having the speed to force the car out there can be misleading. When you do that, you fool yourself into believing you are going as fast as you can because you don't have any more room. Instead, try holding the car as tight as possible (without scrubbing speed or "pinching" it) when you come out of the corner so you have an accurate feel of where that speed takes the car. Then once you feel you are using all the speed and track, you can work on letting the car run free out to the exit point again.

Many small errors can result in a spin, an off-track excursion, or a crash. Most are caused by a lapse in concentration, leading to an error with the controls (usually upsetting the balance, and therefore traction, of the car) or a misjudgment in speed or positioning. The result of the error is usually determined by how calm you stay, and your experience. Learn from your errors.

If the car should start to spin (severe oversteer) once you correct the first slide, be ready for one in the opposite direction caused by overcorrecting. If it happens, gently correct for it by looking and steering where you want to go, and smoothly try to ease the speed down until you get the car under control again.

As you know, weight transfer has a great influence on how your car behaves in a skid or slide. Smoothly controlling that weight transfer is the real key to controlling a spin. And, as this is an oversteer situation, just look and steer where you want the car to go.

If the car begins to spin and you can't control it, you are going to spin out completely. Nothing wrong with that, if you stay relaxed, watch where you are going, depress the clutch, and lock up the brakes—and hope that you don't hit anything. That is about all you can do—besides avoiding the spin in the first place.

In fact, many believe this is the best way to really find out if you're driving the limit. So, if you do spin, learn from it.

If you spin, you should immediately hit the brakes, locking them up. This will cause the car to continue in the general direction it was heading before locking the brakes, while scrubbing off speed. At the same time, try to depress the clutch and keep the engine running by blipping the throttle. Ideally, you'll be able to drive away after the spin. Remember the saying, "spin, both feet in"—on the clutch and brake pedals.

And no matter how bad it seems, always look where you want to go. Never give up trying to regain control.

James Weaver says: "You normally only crash when you make several mistakes in quick succession—and don't react to or recognize the first error. If I'm going to spin, I turn into the spin to make it happen faster—and then only lock the brakes at the point I want the car to continue on at a tangent. I drive the car all the way, and then take my hands off the steering wheel if I'm going to hit something."

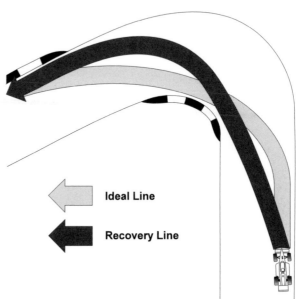

Ideal Line

Recovery Line

If you brake too late or if you are running out of brakes and you find yourself entering a corner too fast, aim the car for a very early apex. This effectively lengthens the distance you have for slowing the car.

In all the excitement of a spin, drivers will often stall the engine when trying to get going again. Take your time, look around to avoid being hit (and watch for signals from the turn marshals), and get going again using lots of engine revs. And remember, your tires may have stones and pebbles stuck to them, severely reducing their grip. So take your time until they clean off, otherwise you'll find yourself spinning again.

On an oval, once you've reached the point in a slide where there is no way you're going to be able to correct it, you have to let it go. If you continue trying to correct it, you will probably spin or drive straight into the wall. You're better off admitting you're going to spin, and let it—it will most likely spin down to the bottom of the track.

What if you enter a turn slightly too fast—to the point where it is impossible to make the car turn-in properly? Most drivers' reaction is to continue braking. But, you'll actually have a much better chance of making the corner if you ease off the brakes slightly. Why? For two reasons:

• The car is better balanced (not too much forward weight transfer), which allows all four tires to work on getting the car around the corner, instead of having the fronts overloaded; and

• Your concentration and attention are on controlling the car at the traction limit as opposed to "getting the car slowed down," or "surviving."

Believe it or not, knowing and using this plan will do more for making you go faster than many other "tricks." You may discover the car will actually go around the corner faster than you thought.

Also, if you are entering a turn too fast (probably because you left your braking way too late), aim for an early apex. This allows you more straight-line braking time to slow the car.

If you run out of track on the exit of a corner (probably due to an early turn-in and apex), you may drop a couple of wheels into the dirt off the edge of the track. If you do, the very first thing to do is straighten the front wheels and drive straight ahead—even if it means driving toward a wall for a few seconds. What this does is allows you time to get the car slowed down and back under control.

If you try to steer the car back on the track immediately, you will most likely end up with the two front wheels back on the pavement and only one rear on. This usually results in a very quick spin back across the track—quite often into another car. Or, if the wheels catch the edge of the pavement at the wrong angle, it may actually "trip" the car, causing it to roll over. Again, keep the front wheels pointing straight until you get the car back in control. Don't panic and "jerk" the car back on the track. It won't work.

Now let's discuss an error that's not necessarily your fault, yet you still have to deal with it: Brake fade.

Brake fade is caused by overheating of various brake components (rotor, pad, caliper, brake fluid). Of course, this may be your fault if you knew this was a weak link in your car's performance and chose to ignore it by overusing the brakes. Sometimes you have to pace yourself to conserve the brakes for maximum use late in a race.

If the brake fade is caused by overheating of the brake pad material (less common these days, unless you're driving a showroom stock vehicle), usually the brake pedal will feel firm. But no matter how hard you press the pedal, the car doesn't slow down much. There is not much you can do except let them cool down by being easy on them for a few laps. Pulling into the pits with hot brakes does very little to cool them. Without any airflow for them, brakes can take a long time to cool. And before they do, they will actually heat up everything else around them— possibly causing even more damage. This is why it's important to do a slow "cool-off" lap at the end of every session.

If the brake fade is caused by overheating (boiling) of the brake fluid (which usually means the rotors and calipers are overheated and are conducting the heat through to the fluid), you will feel a mushy brake pedal—with a lot of pedal travel (perhaps all the way to the floor). Pumping the brake pedal helps build up the pressure in the brake lines—for a while. But again, the only thing you can really do to solve your problem is go easy on them for a few laps to let them cool. Usually, once the fluid has boiled, the firmness of the pedal will not come back without bleeding the system.

Chapter 10

Racing in the Rain

Racing in the rain is obviously a little more dangerous than in dry conditions. Driving smoothly and with full concentration is absolutely critical—it cannot be stressed enough. However, with practice and the right mental attitude, you can gain a great advantage over your competitors.

Personally, I love to race in the rain. Having spent many years in cars that were less than competitive, the rain was my "equalizer." Since wheelspin is the major limiting factor on a wet track, if a competitor's car had more horsepower, the driver usually couldn't use it, therefore equalizing our cars. Also, having spent many years racing in the Pacific Northwest, I've become very accustomed to driving in the rain. Now, my mental attitude toward rain is very positive, but some of my competitors' is negative. While I'm loving it, they're hating it, giving me at least a mental advantage.

The general rule in rain driving is to drive where everyone else hasn't. In other words, off the Ideal Line. The idea is to look for, and use, the grippiest pavement. Through years of cars driving over a particular part of the track, the surface becomes polished smooth and the pores in the pavement are packed with rubber and oil. That is exactly where you don't want to be in the rain. You want to search out the granular, abrasive surface. This can sometimes mean driving around the outside of a corner, or hugging the inside, or even crossing back and forth across the normal line.

SPEED SECRET #21:
Look for and drive the grippiest pavement.

Eventually, of course, you will have to cross the Ideal Line. When you do, try to have the car pointing as straight as possible, so there is less chance for the car to spin.

Since cornering traction is reduced more than acceleration and braking traction in the rain, try driving a line that allows you to drive straight ahead more. That means a later, sharper turn-in and a later apex (see the adjacent illustration).

Often, in a race, the rain will stop and the track will begin to dry. Again, watch for and drive the driest line. This can change dramatically from lap to lap. As the track dries, your rain tires may begin to overheat and tear up. If so, try to drive through puddles on the straights to cool them.

Since water runs downhill, it may be best to drive around the top of a banked

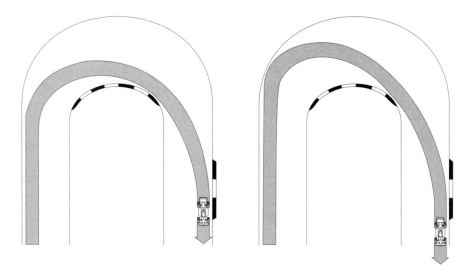

These illustrations show two different lines through the same corner. The illustration on the left is the standard "dry" line; the one on the right is an altered, straighter, "rain" line.

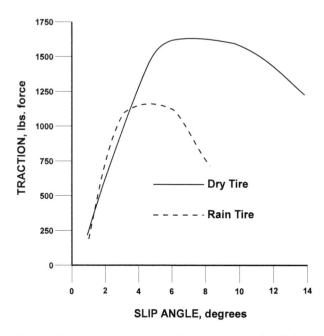

Slip angle versus traction graph for a rain tire and a slick racing tire shows that the rain tire is less "progressive"—it reaches its limit quicker and lets go quicker. Obviously, its traction limit is lower than the dry tire.

corner. Again, search out the pavement that offers better traction. Also, be careful of pavement changes and painted curbing. Often, they are much slicker than the surrounding asphalt.

The optimum slip angle for a tire in the wet is less than in the dry. On dry pavement a tire's optimum slip angle may be in the 6- to 10-degree range; on wet pavement it may be around 3 to 6 degrees. This means you should drive in the rain with the tires slipping less than you would on dry pavement.

This reduced optimum slip angle range also means the line between grip and no grip is a little finer. Plus, once the tires have broken loose and begun to really slide, there is less scrub to slow the car down to a speed where the tires can regain traction. That is why it often feels like a car picks up speed when it spins on a wet track—it's because the rate of deceleration is so little.

A rain tire is usually less "progressive" than a slick. That is, when the rain tire reaches its maximum traction limit (optimum slip angle) and begins to relax its grip on the road, it does so more quickly than the more progressive dry tire. In other words, the rain tire gives you a little less warning as to when it is going to let go (see the accompanying illustration).

These last two factors—the lack of scrub to slow you down when too much slip occurs, and the less progressive nature of the rain tire—is why it is critical to make the car slide from the very instant you enter a turn in the rain. If you try to drive with no slip, at some point the tires are bound to go beyond the "no slip" range and begin to slide. When that occurs, it is going to take you by surprise. You think you've got lots of control . . . it's hanging on . . . hanging on . . . and then suddenly it lets go.

Instead, enter every turn slightly faster than you think possible, and make the car understeer—even if that means little or no trail braking at first. Once it is sliding, keep the car's speed up by squeezing on the throttle. If the car is set up right, you can gently make it go from this understeer to a slight oversteer, always keeping the tires slipping. With a little practice, you'll be able to add your trail braking back in (increasing the initial turn-in speed), and make all four tires slip an equal amount all the way through the turn, using the throttle to control the balance of understeer to oversteer, and therefore control the direction of the car by easing off the throttle to rotate the car, and vice versa.

By having the car slide all the way through the turn, it will never take you by surprise—you know it's sliding.

In fact, the car should be sliding almost all the time. Not too much, mind you, but sliding a smooth, controlled amount.

SPEED SECRET #22:
If the car feels like it is on rails, you are probably driving too slow.

A car on a wet track takes a set in a turn just like it does in the dry. Recall that "taking a set" is that point when all the weight transfer that is going to take place due to cornering force has taken place. In other words, when the car has leaned or rolled in the turn all that it is going to, that is when it has "taken a set." This will happen in the rain just as it does in the dry, only the overall amount of weight transfer will be less due to the lesser amount of cornering force. It may take a little more sensitivity to feel the car take its set.

Having suggested the car should always be sliding, like anything, gradually work your way up to it. Don't try to put the car in large slides all the way through a corner first time out. But don't drive with the car on rails lap after lap either. With each lap, try entering the corner a little faster, and a little faster, until the slipping feels like it is too much, where another .10 mph will mean you can't control the amount of slip.

As you know, how you use the throttle and brake pedal in the dry is critical. Well, it is even more important in the rain. Every time you accelerate out of a corner, feed in the throttle by squeezing the pedal down slower than you would in the dry. If you should ever have to lift off the throttle in a turn, "breathe" it, ease out, "feather" it. Do not lift abruptly. That is probably the most common cause of a spin in the rain. Smooth and gentle—finesse—are the keys to driving in the rain.

You must be smoother on the throttle in the rain—squeezing the throttle so you get just the right amount of wheelspin. Too much and you're either slow (you're not accelerating because of the excessive wheelspin) or you'll spin; too little and you will be slow. Remember the traction limit.

If you get into a little bit of a slide or spin, do as little as possible. It's just like driving over an icy bridge in your street car. There is practically no traction anyway, so whatever you do will have no effect—at least no positive effect, although it can often have a negative effect.

Be very smooth with your shifts. You may want to try driving one gear higher in the turns than you normally would—using third gear in a corner you ordinarily would use second in. This will lessen the chance of severe wheelspin by reducing the amount of torque available to the driving wheels.

Aquaplaning is one of the trickiest parts of racing in the rain—when the tire cannot cut through the buildup of water on the track surface, and it begins to skim across the top of the water. Three factors account for this: the amount of water, the depth and effectiveness of the tread on the tires, and the speed the car is traveling. Be prepared for it whenever it rains heavily.

The trick to controlling aquaplaning is to do as little as possible—be gentle. Aquaplaning is much like driving on ice—the less you do, the better your chances of surviving. Do not take your foot completely off the throttle, as the compression braking effect of the engine and forward weight transfer may cause your rear wheels to slip. Under no circumstances should you hit the brakes. This will only cause you to slide even quicker. Nor should you try to accelerate fully through it.

Turning the steering wheel while aquaplaning can also be dangerous. Imagine "skimming" across the top of a puddle with the front wheels turned at an angle (as if trying to corner). When you reach the other side of the puddle, the front tires will now regain traction, while the rears are still on top of the puddle with no traction. The front end of the car is going to follow the front tires, and the back end is going to skid sideways, causing you to spin out. Therefore, whenever you begin to aquaplane, make sure you're steering straight ahead.

Your chassis/suspension setup may have to be changed for the rain. Generally, you want to run a softer car: softer springs, shocks, and antiroll bars. (In fact, many drivers disconnect the antiroll bars entirely in the rain.) This will help your overall grip while giving you more feel for what the car is doing. If possible, since there will be less forward weight transfer, and therefore braking, by the front wheels, you should adjust the brake bias to the rear. You also may want to add more downforce from the wings, and adjust the tire pressures—less pressure if there is a little rain, more pressure (causing a slight crown across the tread of the tire) in heavy rain to help avoid aquaplaning.

Perhaps the most difficult and dangerous part of racing in the rain is the lack of visibility. When following other cars, you may need to drive just slightly off to either side—not directly behind—to improve your visibility, to avoid the spray and mist. In fact, do everything possible to make sure you have good visibility. Defog and clean your windows and/or helmet visor before driving. There are many antifog products on the market today—some that even work!

James Weaver says: "Lack of visibility is the biggest problem in the rain. In fact, the straightaways—where the rooster tails of the cars in front are the worst—are the most dangerous. I try to look across the corners and count the cars in front before getting on a straight, as they can sometimes be hidden in the balls of spray."

I remember, years ago, reading about Niki Lauda's claim that he was born with a natural advantage in avoiding visor fog-up. Because he has buck teeth, when he breathed in his helmet, his breath went downward away from the visor. From that point on, whenever there was a potential for my visor to fog up, I would concentrate on breathing downward. Plus, I always install a brand new visor on my helmet just prior to driving in the rain. Old visors actually absorb moisture over time and are more susceptible to fogging. It's surprising how much better a new visor is than an old one.

Driving in the rain can be enjoyable, because it's an extra challenge, as long as you concentrate on the changing conditions and drive smoothly and precisely.

Chapter 11

Racing, Passing, and Traffic

Passing, being passed, dicing for position. This is what racing is all about. Some drivers can drive fast but can't race. Others can race but aren't particularly fast. To win, obviously, you must be good at both. And the techniques used to be good at both do not always complement each other.

Having said that, first you must learn to drive fast, then you can begin to race. Many drivers never learn to drive fast because they're too busy racing other drivers. Others are fast, but never really learn how to race—how to pass, defend their position, and so on.

I consider other race cars to be part of the track. Therefore, the race track is constantly changing as their positioning in relation to me changes. You'll be much more successful in your racing if you concentrate on your own performance rather than on the competition. So if you think of the competitors' cars as simply changes in the track layout, you'll be more relaxed and able to achieve your own peak performance.

It's important to be aware of everything and everyone around you—especially in a pack of cars. Train yourself to be very focused, and yet be able to notice other things around you. Practice this on the street. Concentrate on where you are going, but try to make note of all the other cars around you—especially the ones you can't see directly in the mirrors. This ability can make the difference between being just a fast driver and being a great racer. I'll talk more about this "field of awareness" in chapter 14.

No matter what, you are going to have to modify your line when passing and being passed. It's part of racing. Hopefully, though, you can do this to your advantage, not your disadvantage. The goal is to deviate from your Ideal Line as little as possible while passing and being passed.

A good habit to get into during practice sessions is to try driving "passing lines," that is, where you think you may be able to pass competitors in the race. Practice sessions are the time to test the track for grip "off line."

In passing maneuvers, the general racing rule is the overtaking car is responsible for making a clean, safe pass. If the overtaking car is approximately halfway or more past the slower car and on the inside when entering a turn, it is the overtaking car's line. I repeat, though, this is a general rule. The "approximately halfway" is a bit of a gray area.

There are really three ways or places to pass another car:

• By outbraking it while approaching a corner

• Passing on a straightaway (either because your car is faster, you got better acceleration out of the corner leading onto the straight, or by drafting the other car), or

• By passing in a corner (by far the most difficult)

SPEED SECRET #23:
When passing, always "present" yourself.

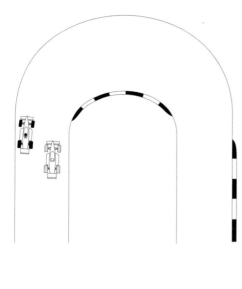

The driver of the car on the inside deserves to have the door shut on him by the car on the outside, for two reasons. First, he hasn't "presented" himself to the other car by getting far enough alongside him. Second, he is too close to the inside edge of the track—too far away from the car on the outside—making it very difficult for the other driver to see him. Instead, he should have eased off the brakes slightly to get farther alongside the other car, and run closer to it as well (a small side benefit of running close to the other car is if the two cars do hit, the impact will be lighter).

Probably the most important aspect of passing is to "present" yourself—making sure you get into a position where your competitor can see you. When you go into a corner on the inside, it is not necessary to pass completely (see the adjacent illustration). Often, if you try to go too deep into a corner to get completely by another car, you overdo it and one of three things happen: you spin, are unable to make a proper turn-in, or you come out of the corner so wide and with so little speed that the other car passes you back on the straightaway (see the adjacent illustration). All you really have to do is get beside your competitor and the line through the corner is all yours. Just match your braking with his. There is nothing he can do about it at that point.

When outbraking a competitor on the inside approaching a corner, do you turn in at the same turn-in point? No. If you did, it would be much too early a turn-in. Instead, continue straight down the inside until you intersect, and then blend in with your usual Ideal Line. That puts you in position to begin accelerating earlier than your competitor.

When following a group of cars into a corner, you most likely will not be able to brake as late as you normally do. As each car in front starts to brake, they begin to "stack" up in front of you. If you tried to go as deep as usual, you would run into the rear of someone.

When trying to pass another car, sometimes you actually have to hang back a little so you can get a run at a part of track where it is easier to pass.

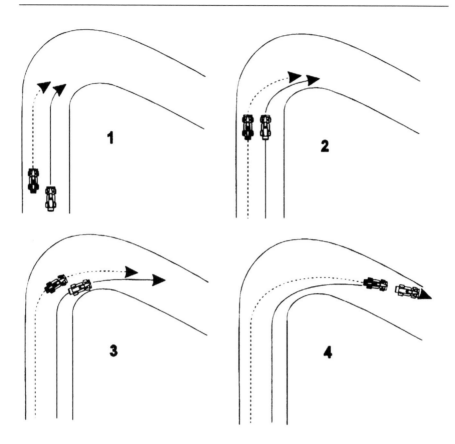

The correct way to outbrake a competitor into a corner. As you can see, all you want to do is get beside your competitor by the time you're at the turn-in point. That way, the corner is yours. The only thing your competitor can do is follow.

You often see a driver in a faster car who cannot pass a slower car because he or she is constantly running into the corner with his or her nose just barely inside the other car. Of course, the driver of the slower car takes the line through the turn and the faster car then needs to slow down as well, losing all its momentum. The driver would have been better off easing back just a little early for the turn, giving the slower car some room, and then accelerating early, driving the corner very hard to gain the momentum down the straightaway—where it is easy to pass.

Remember, anytime you slow slightly while trying to pass another car, you are not at the limit anymore. Therefore, you can probably alter your line to almost anywhere on the track without being concerned about spinning.

If you and another car just in front of you are passing another car, con-

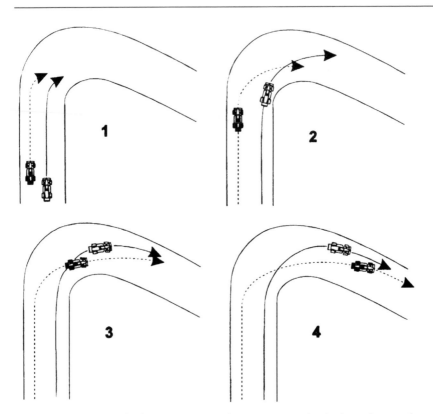

The wrong way to outbrake a competitor. If you get too enthusiastic and go too far past your competitor, it opens the door for him/her to repass you on the exit of the corner. This will probably be easily done, as you have gone too fast into the corner, cannot get back on line to block him/her, and will not be able to begin accelerating as early as your competitor.

sider that the driver of the car about to be passed probably only sees the first passing car—and not you. Be prepared!

If you are obviously slower than the car behind, you should try to let the car pass. But do so on a straightaway, not in a corner. If you have already entered the corner, you are committed to the line—it is your corner. If you change your line in a corner after you are committed to it, you are going to confuse the faster car behind and possibly put yourself in a dangerous position. Be predictable! Wait until you are out of the corner and on the straight; then point to where you want the other car to pass, and let it by. Pointing is important, but make it one or two quick points, then get your hand back on the steering wheel and concentrate on your own driving.

Blocking is a controversial subject. A general rule is: you can defend your position by altering your line—but only once. If you weave down the straight or

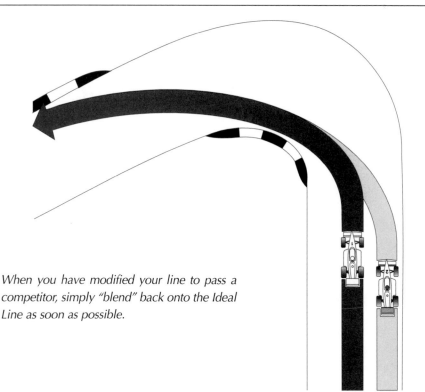

When you have modified your line to pass a competitor, simply "blend" back onto the Ideal Line as soon as possible.

alter your line two or three times on the approach to a corner, that's blocking.

Personally, I don't think blocking is right. Not only is it very dangerous, but if that is what it takes to keep a competitor behind, you don't deserve to be in front. Of course, in the last few laps of a race, almost anything goes—as long as you remember that you're not going to win if both of you crash out of the race. The balance between being a good, aggressive racer and being a blocker is a fine one. Having a reputation as a fair but tough driver is great; having the reputation as a "dirty" driver or blocker usually ends up costing you.

You will learn who you can trust to race wheel-to-wheel. Generally, these drivers will not surprise you by doing something unexpected. They will not suddenly change their line drastically because you're trying to pass. They are predictable. They may change their line slightly to discourage you from trying to pass, but that's to be expected.

Remember, there are no real hard and fast rules regarding passing on the race track. And no insurance on a race car (well, you can get it, but it's very expensive and you still have to pay the deductible yourself, no matter whose fault it is!). So, it takes respect and courtesy for your fellow competitors for all of us to "play" safe.

Chapter 12

Different Cars, Different Techniques?

What about different cars? Are there different techniques required to drive a front-wheel-drive versus rear-wheel-drive car? The answer is, yes and no.

While the basic technique is the same, the difference is in the timing and amount of application of the technique, and the slight variations in the Ideal Line discussed earlier.

In fact, there may be just as much difference between two rear-wheel-drive cars (a Formula Ford and a Trans-Am car, for example) as there is between a front-wheel-drive and rear-wheel-drive.

The biggest difference with a front-wheel-drive car is this: The front tires are doing all the work—steering, accelerating, and most of the braking. Therefore, it's very easy to overload or overwork them. If you overwork the front tires, they will overheat and lose even more traction.

With a front-wheel-drive car you have to be very careful while accelerating in a corner. If you get on the throttle too hard, you overwork the front tires' traction limit while causing a serious rearward weight transfer, resulting in extreme understeer. Be smooth with the throttle—squeeze rather than smash.

Since a front-wheel-drive car has a tendency to understeer (due to all the weight over the front end), it's important to trail brake a little more on the entrance to corners. Left-foot braking is used by many front-wheel-drive racers to help with this trail braking. As well, you may have to use "trailing throttle oversteer" to control the understeer in the middle of a long corner. This means quickly easing off, or "trailing" off, the throttle in the middle of the corner to cause forward weight transfer, reducing the understeer.

With rear-wheel drive, you can kick the rear around tight corners with power oversteer by quickly applying lots of throttle. If you try this with a front-wheel-drive car, all you'll do is increase the understeer.

Some say you must be more precise—that there's less room for error—when racing a front-wheel-drive car. Definitely, you can't be as harsh with the throttle to help overcome an error, as that will usually overload the front tires.

You may want to try to straighten the front wheels a little sooner when exiting a corner with a front-wheel drive, as the limit of how much throttle you can give while the wheels are turned may be less due to the additional forces on the front tires. Usually, a later apex is required. And you know what to do to drive a later apex.

The key to being a versatile driver is being able to adjust or modify your style or technique to best suit the slight variations of different types of cars.

Chapter 13

Flags and Officials

The final parts of the track, but no less important ones to discuss, are the flags and officials. Pay strict attention to the flags the flag marshals show you. They are there to assist you, to help you go as fast as possible, and to ensure your safety.

At practically every race track you'll ever race at, the flag marshals and officials are there as volunteers. They are there for the same reason you are—they love racing. Often, a flag marshal is doing it because he or she can't afford to race yet, and this is better than spectating. Without flag marshals and officials, you will not be able to race. Remember that. Don't think of flags, flag marshals, and officials as hindrances. Think of them as a way to gain an advantage.

Before you first venture onto the race track as a driver, it is absolutely critical that you know and understand what every flag means and how it is used. Take the time to read and understand the rule book that you'll be racing under as the use or interpretation of a flag has been known to change or vary. Keep up to date with the latest regulations.

It's important to not only note and obey all flags, but also to "read" the flag marshals. You can really work this to your advantage. With experience, you will notice differences in the way the marshals wave a flag. If, for example, a marshal is calmly waving a yellow flag (meaning caution, slow down, there is an incident in the vicinity), it's probably not a serious incident. While your competitors are slowing up a lot, you back off a little, gaining a bit of an advantage on them. However, be prepared to slow down. And if the marshal is frantically waving a yellow flag, slow down a lot.

Having said that, remember that flag marshals risk their lives to make racing safer for you. Don't ever do anything that puts them in any greater danger than they already are. And understand that when you slow down 20 or 30 miles per hour from your racing speeds, it may seem to you like you're almost stopped. But, you're probably still traveling at a very high speed with a flag marshal on or near the track assisting another driver.

No matter how much an official's or flag marshal's decision or action seems to be against you, try to accept it and get on with your racing. If you are sure you're being wrongly treated, take it up in the proper fashion (again, read the rule book to learn the proper procedure). Don't take it out on them personally. That will only make matters worse.

The officials are only doing their job, and the better you get along with them, the more successful and enjoyable your racing will be. Often, if over a period of time you have treated the officials with respect, it may even help sway a decision in your favor.

PART 3

The Driver

Driving a race car at any speed is a very complex task. It requires thousands of decisions, reactions, and skills—both physical and mental—in a very short period of time. To win in racing requires even more: a perfectly matched, balanced, controlled, and trained set of mental skills and state of mind, along with the necessary physical techniques and skills.

In this section, we'll examine what I believe is the real secret to winning races. Not how to trick the car up to make it go faster, not how to find the trick line through a corner, but how to find the trick inside of you to help you perform at your maximum level.

Chapter 14

A Racing Mind

Driving a race car is a series of compromises. The Ideal Line for a particular corner may vary slightly from lap to lap, due to rubber buildup or oil on the track, the position of competitors around you, or how your car's handling changes as the fuel load is reduced. You constantly have to monitor and adjust your driving to best suit the condition of your tires. You have to consider and reconsider practically every lap what your race strategy should be. There are hundreds, perhaps thousands, more compromises and decisions to be made every lap.

The driver who chooses the best compromises is most often the winner. A driver whose mind is best prepared is more likely to make the ultimate compromises.

Mental Preparation

Mental preparation for racing, as in any sport, is a key element. All the skills and techniques in the world are not going to make you a winner if you are not properly prepared mentally.

Your mental approach to driving may just have the single biggest effect on your success. What you do to prepare mentally before a practice session or race is somewhat individual. It's difficult for me to tell you what will work for you. You have to experiment to find out for yourself what works and what doesn't. For some drivers, sitting alone, not talking with anyone is the trick, whereas for others, that results in more nervousness. Some prefer talking with friends or their crew to take their mind off the pressure of the next practice, qualifying session, or race.

I strongly suggest giving yourself a few minutes immediately before each session to visually drive the track (more on this shortly), seeing the changes and adjustments to the technique you've planned. In fact, prior to every session, plan out what you're going to change. Laps around a race track are valuable. Make them count. Make a plan and then work on that plan.

Now, the obvious: as a race driver, your goal is constantly to strive to go faster . . . faster than all your competitors. That's all it takes to win!

However, once you've decided you need to go faster (and who doesn't?), and how you're going to go about it, consider everything that could happen. The car may not turn-in when entering the corner 1 mile per hour faster, it may begin to oversteer during the transition phase because of unbalance and too much speed, and so on. This enables you to be mentally prepared for the consequences. This also helps your confidence level because you have it under control—it doesn't take you by surprise. But, don't dwell on it.

In fact, focusing on negative thoughts or ideas will most likely slow you down. Thoughts like, "If I go this much faster, I'm going to crash," takes some concentration and attention away from the ideal, positive thought, like: "I can enter the turn 1 mile per hour faster."

To go faster, you should have an open mind about learning more: about how to improve your driving, about new techniques, about how to make the car go faster, to constantly strive to go quicker and quicker. It's definitely one of the most enjoyable challenges in the world.

Getting advice from more experienced drivers, or other knowledgeable individuals, is good practice. Many drivers will be flattered that you chose to talk to them and will respect you for making the effort to improve.

Talk to and watch successful drivers. Even reading biographies of the best drivers in the world can help. Analyze what they are doing and saying. Obviously, you can't believe everything they say, but listen and analyze for yourself. Many times they are not intentionally trying to lead you astray with wrong advice, but they may not actually know what it is that makes them successful. That's why it's important to watch for yourself and really think about all the aspects that come into play. Watch how other drivers take a particular corner that may be a problem for you. They may have found the secret you haven't. But be careful—they may be worse than you! Check their times and talk to some of the more experienced drivers.

When watching other drivers, notice the line they take and the "attitude" or balance of the car. Ask yourself why the car or driver is doing what it is doing. Understand the strategy and technique being used.

A word of warning, though: Listen to the advice, but you be the judge. Just because it works for someone else doesn't mean it will for you or your car.

State of Mind

You must control your emotional or mental state of mind if you want to be successful. If you are excited, nervous, depressed, stressed, distracted, angry, or whatever, you may not be mentally effective. Your decision making will be slowed, your mind will not be focused.

You don't need to be psyched up. You need to be calm, relaxed, and focused. Psyching up usually makes you overly excited and, therefore, less effective. You want to drive with a clean mind, not one cluttered with useless thoughts.

Once you get into the car, it doesn't matter what is happening outside the car. All that matters is you, the car, the track, and other competitors. Forget everything else. I think this is why many drivers find racing so relaxing. They can forget absolutely everything else that is happening in their lives.

Motivation

If you want to be fast, if you want to win, you must be motivated. No matter how much talent you have, you will never be a consistent winner if you lack motivation. If you want to win races, you have to be "hungry." You have to want it more than anything else.

It's important to identify for yourself why you want to race. And then, do you want to win? What is it about the sport that you enjoy? Be honest. It doesn't matter what it is. What does matter is, once you've identified it, then focus on it. To be motivated, you must love what you are doing. Remember and relive what you love about racing. If that doesn't motivate you, nothing will.

Understand, if you want to win, you will have to take some risks. You almost have to decide how much risk you're willing to accept. If you're not motivated, I'll bet you're not willing to accept very much risk.

If anyone ever tells you they never have any fear in a race car, they either are lying or are driving nowhere near the limit. There's not a successful driver in the world who doesn't scare themselves every now and then. Fear—or self-preservation—is the only thing that stops you from crashing every corner. If it's the kind of fear that makes you panic and freeze up, then that's not good. But if it's the kind that makes the adrenaline flow, your senses sharpen, and makes you realize if you go another tenth of a mile per hour faster you'll crash, then that's good.

Really, it's more of a sense of self-preservation. Usually, you are going much too fast to be scared at the moment. However, there are times when I realize after a corner just how close I was to crashing—and there's a little fear there, knowing I came oh-so-close to losing it. That usually means I was at or a little beyond the limit.

Performance versus Competition

As I mentioned in chapter 11 about passing, you're going to be more successful if you concentrate on your own performance rather than on the competition.

SPEED SECRET #24:
Focus on your own performance rather than on the competition.

Many drivers become too focused on what their competitors are doing. They're constantly looking at what the competition is doing to their cars, observing how they are driving a particular corner, and watching the mirrors to keep them behind.

Instead, if they would put that much focus and concentration on their own car and driving, they would probably be so far ahead they would never have to worry about the competition.

Concentrate and work on getting 100 percent out of yourself and your car. Don't worry about the competition. If you're getting 100 percent out of yourself, you can't do much else about the competition anyway. If you don't win, you can only improve your car's performance level—or work at raising your own 100 percent. After all, your 100 percent today may be only 90 percent six months from now, because your technique has improved. And you can always improve.

Vision

At least 90 percent of your responses and actions in a race car are a result of the feedback you receive from your eyes and what they report to your brain. Although you use your hands, arms, legs, and feet to control the car, it's what your eyes tell your brain that enables them to take action. Therefore, good vision techniques are critical to driving a race car.

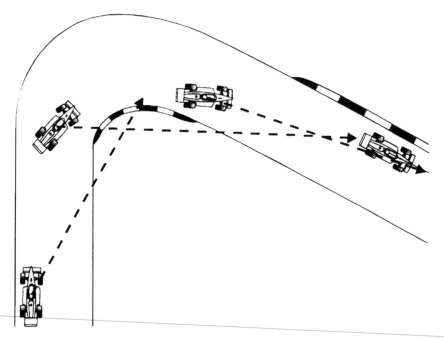

As you enter a corner, before you even get to the turn-in point, you should be looking at and through the apex. You have to know where you're going before you can know how much to turn the steering wheel at the turn-in point. Look as far through the corner as possible.

There is a difference between good vision and good eyesight. Eyesight can be measured—and corrected with glasses if necessary. Vision is the act of sensing with the eyes. Good vision is something that can be practiced.

This may sound obvious but look where you want to go, not where you don't want to go. Why? Because your car will go wherever you look—wherever you focus your eyes.

SPEED SECRET #25:
Focus your eyes where you want to go, not where you don't want to go or where you are.

Focus on and visualize the line you wish the car to follow through a corner, constantly trying to see through the turn to the exit. Many drivers spend far too much time (which is any amount of time—even a fraction of a second) focusing on where they don't want to go, such as the curbs, walls, and other things off the edge of the track. And that's where they usually end up.

In fact, this is the key to driving the Ideal Line. If you want the car to follow a particular line through a corner, then that's where your eyes should be focused. If you don't want the car to go somewhere—like toward a cement wall on the outside of the track—then don't focus there.

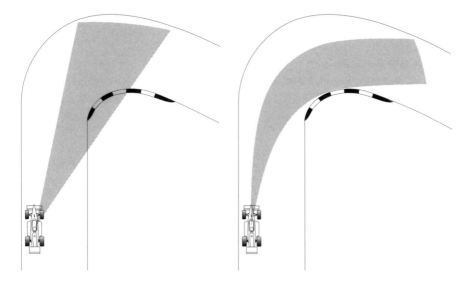

As you approach most corners, what you can actually see is often restricted, and the view your eyes give is straight ahead of where they are pointed (left). But you have to see a curved view around the turn in your mind's eye (right); visualize or picture in your mind the path you want the car to follow.

Just because the car is pointing in a certain direction doesn't mean that's where you want to go. For example, when approaching a corner the car is pointing straight ahead. But where you want to go is into the corner, not straight ahead. So, look through the corner, look for the apex and beyond. That probably means consciously turning your head in that direction. The car will then follow.

Looking where you want to go is only part of it. I learned this while teaching a student—I told him to look where he wanted to go. He got to the turn-in point and abruptly turned the steering wheel toward the inside of the corner—where he was looking. What I failed to tell him—and what I teach now—is to look where you want to go, but have a mental "vision" of the path or line to get there. That's what makes for a smooth arc through a turn.

The better you know the course layout, the better prepared you will be. Always look ahead, planning your route through the corners. If you mess up a particular turn, forget it, and keep looking ahead to the rest of the track. It really doesn't matter where you currently are, so don't look there. What is happening now on the race track was determined by what you did a long time ago. Look now, and plan now, for where you want to go.

SPEED SECRET #26:
Look—and think—as far ahead as possible.

It takes practice to feel comfortable looking farther ahead than you do now, so begin practicing it on the street. You will be amazed at how much it will help—and at how far ahead the winners are looking.

As you drive through the corners, keep your head upright. Many drivers wrongly feel they have to lean their head into the corner to be successful. The weight of your head leaning to the inside of the corner is not going to benefit the handling at all! Watch the best motorcycle racers—even as they lean their bodies into the corner, their heads are cocked as upright as possible. That's because they realize their brain is used to receiving information from their eyes in the normal, upright position, not tipped at an angle. So sit up and keep your head in a normal position. When you turn, move your head from side to side, but do not lean or tip it.

Do not concentrate on just one car in front or behind you. Look well ahead, and watch for anything coming into your overall field of vision. Pay attention all the time. And don't just look farther ahead, think farther ahead.

The best race drivers have a tremendous ability to know what's going on around them without having to look. Call it a sixth sense, or extraordinary peripheral vision, but it is amazing what a driver notices when driving at speed—with experience. Like a person's field of vision, I call this a driver's "field of awareness"—what you are aware of.

Do you remember the first time you drove very fast, or skied down a mountain? Your field of vision, or awareness, was probably very small—like looking through a scope. But the more you drove quickly or skied, the more your vision expanded, and the more you noticed around you.

Personally, there are times when I notice things to the side or behind me that physically I shouldn't know anything about. But with the adrenaline flowing, my senses are so sharp that I know exactly where a car behind me is, even though the view in the mirror is almost nonexistent.

When I first drove an Indy car, my field of awareness was narrowed by the speed at which everything was happening (just as it was when I first drove a Formula Ford, and then a Formula Atlantic car). But as I became more accustomed to the speed, the more my field of vision and awareness expanded once again.

Experience in a fast car—at high speed—will help you become acclimatized to this speed, and increase your "field of awareness." But, it is something you can also practice while driving on the street. Work on seeing and being aware of everything around you at all times. Use your mirrors and peripheral vision to keep track of cars behind and beside you, trying to anticipate what they are going to do.

This ability to know what's going on around you is one of the most important, and amazing, feats race drivers accomplish. If a driver has to think about it while driving, it won't work. But when it's there, it's not only a great feeling, but also a real key to success. It will come with experience if you allow it.

All these things—focusing your eyes on where you want to go, looking far ahead, and using your peripheral vision—are what good vision techniques are all about.

Comfort Zone

Related to the "field of awareness" is your comfort zone. When you first start racing, in whatever type of car you choose, it feels very fast. In fact, it's almost as if you can't keep up. But, with experience, you become more comfortable and accustomed to the speed and feel of the car. I call this your comfort zone.

When you progress up to a faster car, you're once again having to push the limits of your comfort zone. But again, with experience, your comfort zone expands and you feel confident racing at the new speeds.

Some drivers adapt more quickly to faster cars than others. This doesn't necessarily mean they are better drivers, just that they can expand the limits of their comfort zone quicker.

When I first drove a ground-effects car, I had to work on expanding my comfort zone—building my confidence. With a ground-effects car, the faster you go, the more aerodynamic downforce you have. This gives you more grip, which means you can go even faster. That takes confidence—but it doesn't happen immediately.

The first time I went to Indy, it took a little time to get used to the speed. I hadn't ever run at over 200 miles per hour, and I had to work that speed into my comfort zone gradually.

Often, if you feel as though things are happening too fast, as though you're being rushed, it may just mean you're not looking far enough ahead. Pick up your vision, and your comfort zone will expand.

To drive fast and win races you have to feel totally confident driving at the car's limits. That means your limits—your comfort zone—must be at least equal to the car's limits. In fact, your comfort level must be equal to the car's performance level, otherwise it is next to impossible to drive at 100 percent. Again, this takes experience and constantly pushing the limits of your comfort zone.

Consistency

The mark of a great racer is consistency. If you can consistently lap a track at the limit, with the lap times varying no more than a 1/2 second, then you have a chance to be a winner. If your lap times vary more than that, no matter how fast some of them are, you won't win often.

When you first start racing, concentrate on being consistent. Don't be too concerned with your speed. Work on being smooth and consistent with your technique lap after lap.

To do that, when driving the limit, you must remember what you did, and keep doing it lap after lap. That is not as easy as it sounds. But it's not until you drive consistently that you can begin to work on shaving that last few tenths or hundredths of a second off your lap time.

If you want to change something—either to the car's setup or your driving technique—how are you going to know if it took a few tenths of a second off your lap time if you're not lapping consistently to begin with?

Visualization

Your brain does not distinguish between real and imagined occurrences. Fortunately for you, it sees and accepts all images as if they were real. Therefore, it makes sense to visualize, that is, imagine or mentally practice driving. Not only is it free, but it may be the only place where you can really drive a perfect lap.

In your mind's eye, see yourself repeatedly driving exactly the way you want: driving the perfect line, balancing the car smoothly at the very limit, making a well-executed pass, and so on. Mentally drive the race car. But do it successfully. It's amazing how often an error in a driver's mental visualization of a lap actually happens. So, visualize yourself doing it right!

Visualization, or mental practice, is so very effective for a number of reasons. First, it's perfectly safe. You can never hurt either the car or yourself. Second, you can visualize anywhere. You don't need a race track or a car. And because of that, it's free. I don't have to remind you how important this is!

Next, there's no fear of failure. You always drive perfectly. You can even win every time out if you wish. You can visualize in slow motion. This gives you time to be aware of each minute detail of the technique, perfecting it before heading out on the track.

You can mentally prepare for something that may happen only once a season. But when it does, you're ready for it, and you can respond in the best way possible. For example, you can visualize different scenarios at the start of a race: someone spinning in front of you and you reacting to it; a driver moving to the inside of a corner to block you from passing, and you setting up to accelerate early and pass him on the exit of the corner, and so on.

When I raced Formula Ford, a fellow competitor and I were good friends. We battled really hard with each other on the track—maybe even harder than against other competitors because we could trust each other. Then, after the race was over and before the next one we would spend hours talking about the various passing moves we made, others made, and what we could have done if the situation had been different. We didn't realize it at the time, but we were helping each other visualize racing strategy and techniques. We literally practiced thousands of passes. We drove hundreds of races that season in our minds. The result was, when we were in a race, we made quick, aggressive, decisive passes. And they were easy because we had practiced them so many times. We won a lot of races.

Finally, visualizing prior to heading out onto the track forces you to focus and concentrate.

I used to like to use a stopwatch to time my visualization laps. If I knew the track well, my mental lap times would be within a second of my real lap times. That told me I was visualizing accurately—which meant I was probably going to be very fast.

Of course, before visualizing, you must have some kind of "feel" for what you are doing. There's no point in visualizing yourself driving a car or track you've never actually seen before. Without some prior knowledge, some background information, you may be practicing something the wrong way. Remember, visualizing an error is practicing an error. Practicing an error is a sure way of ensuring you will repeat it.

As you turn into a corner, have a mental picture of where you want to be at the exit. You can't get somewhere if you don't know where it is you're going. In fact, as I mentioned earlier, one of the most common errors—turning in early to a corner—is usually caused by not knowing where you want to be at the exit.

Visualization is programming—programming your mind just like you would a computer. And programming allows you to drive using your subconscious mind instead of your conscious mind.

Subconscious Driving

It is not possible to drive a race car effectively (read: fast, at the limit) by consciously thinking about each movement, maneuver, and technique. A race car is much too fast to allow you the time to think through each and every function. Your conscious mind cannot react and respond quickly enough to operate the controls of a race car at speed. It must be a subconscious act.

To do this, you have to program your mind, just like a computer. How? By practicing, both mentally and physically. At first, it is a conscious act. Your conscious mind tells your right foot to move from the throttle to the brake pedal, your arms to begin arcing the steering wheel into a corner, and so on. But after doing this particular function over and over again, it becomes programmed into your subconscious mind. Then, when required, it just happens automatically, without you actually thinking about it.

It's the same as going to the refrigerator for a drink. You don't have to consciously think to stand up, move your left leg in front of your right leg, the right leg in front of the left, and so on. You've done it so often, it's a subconscious act.

When you drive at a subconscious level, it allows your conscious mind to "watch" what you are doing—to see if there is anything you can do to improve your technique, or sense what the car is doing in terms of handling. As you drive subconsciously—by your "program"—your conscious mind watches, senses, interprets what you and the car are doing, and then makes changes to the "program" (subconscious) to improve. There is no point in continuously driving subconsciously if your program doesn't have you driving at the limit. Your conscious mind must always work at reprogramming or updating your mind's program—your subconscious.

That is why it is important to start off slow when learning a new track or car, and gradually build up your speed. It allows the conscious mind to keep up to the speed of the car, while it programs your subconscious.

There are times when I'm out on the track and I'm not really even thinking about what I'm doing—I'm just driving. I come in and I can't actually remember what I did. Obviously, the car has to be working well or I'll be thinking too much about it, but I will have more concentration on what the car is doing, and therefore be more sensitive to what the car is doing. As I mentioned earlier, this programming can be done with actual physical practice, or by visualizing it. But it does take some time.

One of the most common mental errors a race driver makes is "trying." Trying is a conscious act. Not only is trying not an automatic, programmed act, but the second you try, your body tenses and therefore is unable to perform smoothly. Trying is a primary cause of errors, particularly under pressure. You must learn to relax and let your body and the car "flow." Drive naturally and subconsciously.

Concentration

Concentration is the key to consistency. When you lose concentration, your lap times begin to vary. In my early years, I would always check my lap times after a race to see how much they varied. If I could run each lap in an entire Formula Ford race within 1/2 second of the others, I was happy with my concentration level.

When you physically tire, your concentration level suffers. If you notice your lap times slowed and became erratic near the end of a race, it may be that you became physically tired and began to lose concentration. Many drivers blame the car at this point, claiming the tires "went off," when in fact it was their concentration level that went off.

Many drivers lose concentration when they are running alone, just trying to make it to the finish. That is when it is most important to concentrate. Often, at that point in a race, I find it best to talk myself around the track. What I'm actually doing is reprogramming my mind. Usually after a couple of laps of talking myself around I'm back to driving subconsciously.

There is a limit to how much a driver can concentrate on. During a race, you can easily concentrate too hard on one particular area when you really need to spread it over two or three areas. But when trying to go faster—especially during practice sessions—work on one concentration area at a time.

Don't go out on the track and try to "go faster everywhere." Your brain cannot handle everything at once. Instead, decide on two or three areas at most—two or three of the most important things that will make you faster—and work on them.

It takes more concentration to keep something from happening than it does to make something happen. Don't be concerned with making an error—you should be willing to make errors. The more you concentrate on resisting them (such as keeping the car away from a wall or the edge of the track at the exit of a corner), the more likely it is you will make them. Relax!

Don't let a mistake take your concentration away. Everyone makes mistakes. Learn from them, then forget them. It's important when you make an error on the track to quickly understand why it happened, so you can ensure it doesn't happen again, and then concentrate on what's happening next.

Once in a while, just go and drive without thinking about going faster or worrying about making mistakes—relax and let it flow.

Flow

With experience—or "seat time"—comes flow. This is when you are driving subconsciously and naturally, without trying. Often, after being passed or passing someone, it may be difficult to regain your flow. It's important to concentrate on getting back into the flow—regaining your rhythm. Again, a couple of laps of talking yourself around the track may help.

You know when you're in the flow and when you're not. It feels great when you are. Often, when you're not, it's because you're trying. You can't try to get in the flow. It comes naturally. Just let yourself feel like you're part of the car—one with the car. Everything you do becomes automatic and subconscious—shifting, braking, turning, and so on.

I think everyone has experienced being "in the flow" at some time in their life. It may have been while doing a job, playing a sport or musical instrument, or just going about a normal day. It's that time when everything seems to go right, everything you do works perfectly, almost without thinking about it. Unfortunately, everyone has probably experienced the opposite, when no matter how hard you try, it just doesn't seem to work. And often that's the problem—trying too hard.

Chapter 15

Car Control

Car control is the ability to control the car at the very limit. It is the most important skill a driver can ever learn. The ability to make a car do what you want it to—brake, steer, accelerate, oversteer, understeer, neutral steer, and so on—comes from coordinating all the basic control skills together with the correct timing, precision, and application.

Great car control skills allow you to drive at, and just beyond if you wish, the "theoretical" traction limit. This is where the car is in a slide all the way through the corner, balanced on the very edge of control. However, it's very easy to slide the car too much, which actually slows you down by scrubbing off speed. Remember the examples in the slip angle section in chapter 5.

A lot of this great car control will come with experience—getting comfortable with being able to "throw" the car into a turn, and feeling confident with being able to then catch it at the limit. Of course, this must be done smoothly.

I believe a driver who has great car control skills but who is not driving the Ideal Line through a corner will be faster than a driver with the opposite abilities. Therefore, if you want to go fast, if you want to win, develop your car control skills through practice. Then make sure you are driving the Ideal Line as well—that should be easy.

Fighting the Car

Although driving the Ideal Line is important in terms of maximizing your cornering speed, fighting for perfection may actually slow you down. Don't fight the car, if that's what it takes to make it drive the Ideal Line. If you do, you will actually scrub off more speed than if you drove slightly off-line. Too many drivers fight the car to clip past the perfect apex, only to slow the car down doing it. This shouldn't be an excuse to drive off-line. But, if you do turn in to a corner and realize you are going to be slightly off-line, don't fight it—let the car go where it wants—let it flow through the corner. The car will tell you if you are driving the right line or not. And again, don't "pinch" it into the inside of the turn on the exit—let it run free as you unwind out to the exit.

I remember the first time I drove the Milwaukee oval I learned very quickly that it's better to let the car run where it wants to rather than fight it to run on the theoretical Ideal Line—which was very bumpy at Milwaukee.

Chapter 16

The Limit

Consistently driving the limit—as fast as you and the car can possibly go—is the ultimate goal. So, how do you get to that limit? How do you learn where the limit is? Well, you simply make changes that result in you driving the limit or in lower lap times. And you either make these changes by:

- Analyzing and planning prior to going on the track

and/or

- Trial-and-error experience on the track.

The first may be dangerous if you analyze and plan with misleading information or without having sufficient background, while the second can only be done on the track (which costs money).

One way to analyze and plan is to use a track map. Bear in mind that trying to learn the Ideal Line by studying a diagram can sometimes fool you. Elevation, banking, and track surface changes aren't evident, and the map may not be accurate. This sometimes leads to a misconception of how to drive a corner. Then, before you can actually learn the right way on the track, you have to "unlearn" the preconceived ideas. This can take up a lot of valuable track time, and should be a practice you use only when necessary, and with caution.

A better way to analyze and plan is to do so after you have spent some time on the track. You must be able to observe what you are doing so you can improve on it. Analyze your errors to determine what influenced or caused them. Don't dwell on every single mistake you ever make, but study the decision or action that led to the error to ensure it doesn't happen again.

Observing what you do is the key to learning from your errors. In fact, sometimes you should let small errors happen—learn how a different line works, or doesn't. You should consider that in most cases, by the time you notice a error, it may be too late to correct it anyway. About all you can do then is minimize its effect. In fact, that is the key—minimizing the effect of an error, and doing so as soon as possible.

Mistakes are a natural process—don't fight them. Instead, consider what you can learn from an error, then reprogram or visualize yourself doing it the correct way, and forge ahead.

Learn by observation, appreciation, and imitation. Imitation is the ultimate learning technique. Copying is the most instinctive, simple, and natural way to learn. After all, that's exactly how we learned to do practically everything as children. If you want to learn a skill, find someone who is very good at it. Then watch this person carefully. As you watch, feel yourself moving in the same way; then practice by visually imitating. And that doesn't mean just what the driver is doing in the car. How a driver acts outside of the car is just as important. "Acting as if" you were Michael Schumacher or Michael Andretti outside the car will improve your ability to drive like them.

Even if you aren't able to imitate someone perfectly, your attempts will increase your awareness of what skills, techniques, and mental approach you still need to develop.

Of course, you must first be prepared to imitate someone. Don't try copying the advanced techniques of a world champion before mastering the basics. And remember, every driver's learning curve is different. Some learn and progress quickly, others much slower. This is not an indication as to how much talent a driver has.

Driving the Limit

How do you really know when you're driving right at the very limit, getting the very last ounce of speed out of your car?

Ultimately, and simply speaking, your speed is limited by three things: engine output, aerodynamics, and traction. With more engine output you will be faster on the straights; with more traction you will be able to brake harder on the approach to a turn, go faster through the corners, and accelerate harder coming out of corners; and aerodynamic downforce helps traction while the drag slows you down.

Once you're in the car you can't do much about engine output or the car's aerodynamics, but you may be able to do something about traction. You may not be able to increase the amount of traction your car has, but you can drive so that you use all the traction effectively.

As I mentioned earlier, the more gradually you turn in to a corner, for example, the more traction the tires will have since a tire's traction limit will be higher if you progressively build up to it. Balancing the car will increase your usable traction.

Once again, when driving the limit, you are actually dealing with three different limits: The Car, The Track, and yourself (The Driver). You must recognize and maximize each if you are to go faster. Although there isn't anything you can do about changing the track's limit, and raising the car's limits is for mechanics and engineers—with your input of course—maximizing your limits is something to strive for.

Let's go back to the beginning, to the obvious. Driving at the limit means having the tires at their very limit of adhesion (traction) at all times—during braking, cornering, and acceleration. Think for a moment of dividing up your driving into those three phases: braking, cornering, and acceleration. Now, we know that with most cars, we are nowhere near the limit of traction during acceleration at anything above first gear (in how many cars can you spin the tires consistently in second, third, fourth, or fifth gear?). This makes the acceleration phase fairly simple.

However, remember from my previous comments about the Traction Circle that there should be an overlap of the three phases. Overlapping the acceleration and cornering, and even more so the braking and cornering, is where the skill comes into play.

To drive the very limit, you must brake as late as possible at the traction limit all the way to the corner turn-in point, then as you begin the cornering phase, ease off the brakes (overlapping the braking and cornering to keep the tires at their traction limit) until you are at the cornering limit. At this point, you begin squeezing on the acceleration while unwinding the steering (again overlapping cornering and acceleration to stay at the limit of traction).

Now, if all this is done properly, you will be driving the car at the very limit of adhesion. And remember, at the limit, the tires are actually slipping a certain amount, so don't worry if the car is sliding through the corner. It should be. As you are driving through the corner, the car should be sliding slightly, with you making very, very small corrections to the brakes, steering, and throttle to keep the tires at their optimum slip angles, or traction limits.

But your traction limit may not be as high as the next driver's. Why? Because you may not be balancing the car as well as the other driver. Remember that the better the car is balanced (keeping the weight of the car equally distributed over all four tires), the more overall traction the car will have. So, it is possible for you to drive your car at your limit and still have someone else drive your car faster. Or, your limit can be higher than someone else's. It all comes down to balancing the car.

For example, did you ever wonder why, when they were teammates, Ayrton Senna was often quicker than Alain Prost? It wasn't because Senna's car was faster, or that he was braver, or drove a better line through the corner. It's certainly not because Prost wasn't driving his own limit. It was because Senna was able to balance the car so delicately, so perfectly, that his limit of traction was slightly higher than Prost's. That allowed him to enter the corner at a fraction of a mile per hour faster, and begin accelerating a fraction of a second sooner, meaning he was also faster down the straight.

You are receiving information from the car at all times. The more sensitive you are to receiving that feedback, the better you will be able to drive the car at the very limit. People always talk about the feedback a driver gets through the "seat of his pants." Well, I don't know about you, but I have many more nerve endings in my head than in my rear end!

You receive more information through your vision than through any of the other senses (smell and taste have relatively little to do with race car driving; hearing does play a role; and feel is certainly important, but not as important as vision).

Imagine yourself looking at the roadway just over the nose of the car. If the car begins to oversteer you will be looking in a very slightly different direction. But if you were looking farther ahead—almost to the horizon—you would notice a much larger change in sight direction. In other words, the farther ahead you look, the more sensitive you will be to very slight changes in direction, or sliding of the car. Much of the feel of driving comes from your vision.

But how do you really know if you are driving the limit? The only way to know for sure is to go beyond it every now and then. That can be a little hard on equipment—unless you are able to go beyond the limit and still catch it before you end up in the weeds. That's the tricky part.

In fact, before you can consistently drive at the limit, you have to be able to drive beyond the limit. Think back to the four hypothetical drivers in the slip angle section of chapter 5. Remember how the second driver would drive beyond the ideal slip angle range, and the car ended up sliding more than what was optimum for maximum traction. No, that was not the fastest way to drive, but you have to be able to do that before you can really know where the limit is. Once you've driven beyond the limit—and kept the car on the track, somewhere near the Ideal Line—it is much easier to dial it back a little, back to "at the limit." If you can't overcompensate, or overdrive, you'll never be able to home in on the limit. If you can't over-drive a car, you'll never be able to drive the limit consistently.

When you're driving an Indy car, with its extremely high limits, it takes a little time to determine exactly where those limits are. It wasn't until I had progressed to the point where I could consistently drive an Indy car beyond the limit that I felt that I was able to get the most out of it. In other words, I believe a driver must be able to push the car beyond the limit before he can ever drive at the limit on a consistent basis.

At the Detroit Indy car race in 1994, I was driving a '92 Lola with the Chevy Ilmor "A" engine—about 100 horsepower or more down on the rest of the field. In the first qualifying session I ran a time that the team was happy with—faster than we had gone the year before in the same car. But, the car was pushing (understeering) a little, so I knew there was more in it.

For the second qualifying session I left the car alone, didn't try to adjust the understeer out. All I did was concentrate on driving—entering the turns a little quicker, trail braking a little deeper, getting on the power earlier in each corner, and hustling the car between turns—being aggressive but smooth. I ended up taking another full second off my previous day's time. And the car wasn't pushing anymore, it was loose (oversteering).

Two points here. First, I didn't try to make too many changes to the car. I knew there was more in me—I had to concentrate on my driving, not the car. If I had tuned out some of the understeer, when I got going faster, the oversteer would have made the car undrivable. I knew that as more rubber was put down on the track, it would get grippier. And I knew as I drove faster and worked the tires more, the fronts would grip better.

Second, I never put a limit on how fast I thought I could go. Even though the time I turned in the first qualifying session was as fast as most people thought was possible for our old car, I wasn't going to believe that was the limit. I kept thinking there was more. It was a valuable lesson. There are many times when you think you're driving as fast as your car can go—sometimes, because that's as fast as anyone else has gone in a similar car. You can't set limits on yourself. Always believe there is more.

At every corner on every lap you want to strive to brake as late as possible. Where is that? At the last possible moment and still be able to get the car to turn in properly. Many drivers make the mistake of braking so late they can't get the car to turn into the corner correctly.

Enter each corner at a speed slightly above what you think is the limit, then make the necessary corrections to balance the car as it slides through the rest of the corner, while beginning to accelerate as early and as hard as possible (still gently to keep the car balanced) to maximize straightaway speed. It may be easier to do than it is to explain.

Oh yes, and don't forget to drive the absolute perfect Ideal Line—or at least within a quarter of an inch of it. Many drivers can do this for one corner, or one lap. But to do this consistently lap after lap is the goal. You can drive the limit on the wrong line—but you're not going to be a winner!

The difference between a slow driver and a fast driver is that the slow driver is not consistently driving at the very limit all the way around the track. The difference, then, between a fast driver and a winner is that the winner drives consistently at the limit on the Ideal Line.

I have my own little mental check to see if I'm driving the limit. If I ever felt as though I could turn the steering wheel a little more—tighten the radius—at any point in the corner, without causing the car to spin or slide more, then I knew I wasn't driving at the very limit. Next lap, I would try a little faster—to push it a little closer to the limit.

Chapter 17

Going Faster

We're now entering the area for more experienced racers. Once you perfect the basics, you'll no doubt be asking yourself, How can I go faster? If you could only get an answer that would shave a few fractions of a second off your best time, you would be a happier driver. The following thoughts and ideas might help you figure out how to do so.

During my Rookie Orientation at Indy, Rick Mears explained his method for going faster, an approach I've followed ever since. To go faster you should inch up on the limit, going a little bit quicker each lap until you feel you're going beyond the limit—taking little bites of speed to reach the limit rather than taking large bites. If you take big bites of speed, you may go from just below the limit to way beyond in one step.

When trying to go faster, don't use negatives like "Why can't I take that corner faster?," "I didn't brake hard enough," or "I didn't have a good line through that corner." Instead, ask yourself positive, constructive questions like "Where can I go faster?" and "How much faster can I take turn four?"

A driver needs more of a plan than "I'm going to take turn four faster." You must have a plan for how you are going to take turn four faster. After each session, sit down and think it through. Look at a map of the course and visualize yourself driving it as you just did, making notes on areas where you may be able to improve. Think about what you're doing at and during each corner's reference points and control phases: braking, turn-in, trail braking, transition, balanced throttle, apex, progressive throttle, maximum acceleration, and exit. Then ask yourself how you can change what you are doing to go faster.

Corner entry speed is critical. If it is not correct, you spend a lot of time and concentration trying to make up for the incorrect speed. But you need as much of your concentration as possible to sense traction, balance, and the line at this point. Following the advice "enter the corner slow and come out fast" can actually cause problems. I know I gave you this advice earlier—and it's still true. However, you can take it too far. It's possible to enter the corners too slowly. Then, as you accelerate to get up to the correct speed, you exceed the traction limit of the driving tires and get wheelspin. As a result, you're slow, even though it feels as if you're at the limit because of the wheelspin. Plus, once you've realized you are entering the turn too slowly, it takes time to react and correct your speed.

It's important not to slow the car too much with the brakes on the approach to a corner. Remember the saying, "brakes are like lawyers—they cost you every time you use them." Every time you slow the car with the brakes, you have to work hard at regaining your speed or momentum.

Let's look at an example. If a corner could be entered at 52 miles per hour, and you slow to 50 miles per hour at the entrance and then try to accelerate back up to 52 miles per hour, you may exceed the driving tires' traction limit—resulting in power oversteer with a rear-drive car, or power understeer in a front-driver. If you had entered the corner at 52 miles per hour, you wouldn't have to make up for the error in speed. The change in speed wouldn't have been so drastic.

In fact, the more you slow the car at the entry of the turn and the longer you wait to get back on the throttle, the more likely you'll want to make up for the lack of speed by accelerating hard—probably too hard. That results in demanding too much from the driving tires, leading either to power oversteer or power understeer. Again, the change in speed is too extreme.

Racing in the rain taught me a very valuable lesson—one I use in the dry as well. I found that if I purposely made the car slide slightly from the very second I entered the turn I was automatically smoother and more relaxed, and therefore faster. This is because I had no fear of the car suddenly taking me by surprise by starting to slide. I was operating within my comfort zone. The moment I learned this, I started winning races.

You should aim to enter the turn just slightly faster than the traction limit dictates (as long as you can still make the car turn in to the corner properly), so the car slides (scrubs) while you are transitioning off the brakes over to the throttle to begin acceleration. This accomplishes two things:

• While the car is scrubbing a little speed, it allows you time to transition to the throttle without wasting speed (instead of having the car lose speed while you sense you are going too slow, and then having to react and try to correct your speed), and

• It mentally prepares you for the slide so it doesn't take you by surprise.

Don't judge your corner entry speed by your mistakes. Just because the car wouldn't turn in at 52 miles per hour doesn't necessarily mean that's too high a corner entry speed. It may just be that it's too fast for the way you've balanced the car and the way you've turned the steering wheel into the corner. Try working on your corner entry technique for a while, trying to get the car to turn in at 52 mph—or even faster.

Remember that most of the time the fastest straightaway speed comes on laps with the fastest midcorner speeds. To have a fast midcorner speed, you need to enter the corner as fast as possible—at the limit.

This is another one of those compromises you need to make in your driving—

deciding whether you're better off entering a corner slightly slower and getting on the throttle earlier, or carrying more speed into the corner. Usually, if your increase in corner entry speed delays when you begin to accelerate in the corner, you are better off slowing down slightly to get back on the throttle early.

When trying to go faster, work on problem areas and leave strong points alone. Work on one thing at a time. Record all lap times, and have someone take segment times to determine where you are fast and where you are not. Divide the track up into segments, and time yourself and others through them. This will determine where you are gaining and where you are losing.

When I'm learning a new track or car, I concentrate on finding the big chunks of time first, trying to improve two or three pieces at a time. There is no point in going out on the track and trying to go faster everywhere. The mind can't handle too much information at one time. I pick two or three places on the track where I think the largest gains can be made. And I work on only them until I've gotten them dead on, then I pick two or three new places or things to work on. Any more than three and my brain tends to go into overload. Of course, it's the final little pieces of time that are the hardest to find.

Making changes to the car is one obvious way of going faster. It's also a way of going slower. Don't fool yourself. Don't pretend to feel a chassis or aerodynamic change if you don't, just to make it look like you know what you're doing. Not every change is noticeable. (We'll talk more about this in the next chapter.)

And don't make changes to the car before knowing the track and getting into a flow. Take your time. Make sure you are consistently driving at the limit before making drastic changes. That way, you'll know if it's the car or you that's making the difference.

Anything you can do to increase the time spent at full throttle is a good thing. Even if it's for a fraction of a second between two turns, or instead of slowly trailing off the throttle at the end of a straightaway you come off the gas quickly (not forgetting smoothness). That's "hustling" a car.

SPEED SECRET #27:
Your right foot should either be on the brakes, squeezing the throttle down, or flat to the floor.

When trying to shave that last few tenths or hundredths of a second off your lap time, you really have to look at where you are not hustling the car. This is in those very short little sections on the track where you think 80 percent throttle is good enough. To be a winner, "good enough" just won't cut it. You have to use 100-percent throttle—flat out. You also have to be aggressive with the car—smooth, but aggressive. You have to attack the track.

The type of corners that drivers have the most problem with are the really fast ones—the ones that should be taken flat, at full throttle. I learned a trick at Indianapolis that has helped me deal with this type of corner at any track.

The real problem with fast corners is that the car works best—it's balanced with good grip—when you are flat on the throttle all the way through the turn. If you're on and off the throttle, or even progressively squeezing on the throttle through the turn, the car often feels uncomfortable—it hasn't taken a set and therefore has less grip. However, taking a really fast corner flat out right away requires a lot of confidence, so most drivers lift just prior to the corner. And that's what upsets the car's balance. It takes a lot of practice to be able to drive into the corner without lifting.

At Indy, I was told of another approach and have used it a lot since. At first, ease out of the throttle well before the corner on the straightaway to reduce speed enough to make you confident. Then, get back on full throttle prior to turning into the corner, and continue flat through the turn. This way, the car is balanced and very comfortable through the corner. With each lap, gradually reduce the amount of lift before the corner, until you're able to take the turn without lifting at all.

To end this chapter, let's take a look at three specific plans (there are thousands) to go faster.

• The Late Braker: For the average racer this is the most common, and most overused, technique. Most drivers think that by going a little deeper into the corner before braking, they will gain a lot by maintaining the straightaway speed longer. It's only natural to think this way. After all, when running side-by-side with another driver, whenever you brake later you end up in front.

However, in reality, by braking later most drivers brake harder than before, meaning the car enters the turn at the same speed as before. Just braking later, while not carrying more speed into the corner, will gain you very little. All it does is maintain your top speed for a few feet longer on the straight. This is okay for picking up a few hundredths of a second, but not much more. Carrying more speed into the corner (as long as you can still make the car turn in and accelerate through the turn) will make a much bigger improvement.

Consider this: On an average roadracing circuit if you can enter each corner even 1 mile per hour faster, you will have made up to a 1/2-second improvement in your lap time. That's a huge gain.

The big problem with late braking, though, is that you end up focusing too much on braking, when you really should be concentrating on more important things. In fact, quite often you've focused so much on the braking that you overreact and lock up the brakes. Usually, you've left your braking so late that all you're doing is thinking about surviving instead of thinking about braking correctly and what you have to do when you're finished braking.

• The Light Braker: This is usually the first step in the right direction in trying to go faster. You brake at the same point as before, but with a slightly lighter brake application. This means you will carry more speed into the corner (remember, if you can carry just one extra mile per hour, you will have a great reduction in lap time).

• The Late, Correct Braker: This is the goal. You brake later than previously, but at the original (threshold) braking rate. So now you gain by maintaining your top speed on the straight longer (small gain), as well as carrying more speed into the corner (big gain). And you haven't spent all your concentration solely on braking—you are thinking about corner entry. That's how to go faster! Remember, of course, there is a limit.

Chapter 18

Driving Style

The driving styles of the greatest racers in the world have one thing in common. Jackie Stewart, Alain Prost, and Ayrton Senna in Formula One, Mario Andretti, Al Unser Jr., and Rick Mears in Indy car racing, or Richard Petty, Darrell Waltrip, and Dale Earnhardt in NASCAR—the key to their success has always been smoothness and finesse (even if it doesn't always look like it—especially in the rough-and-tumble world of NASCAR).

With experience you will develop your own driving style, one that suits your personality and your car. Everyone, in fact, has their own driving style. Hopefully, yours will be one of smoothness and finesse as well.

Because of individual driving styles, a car setup for one driver may not suit you completely. If, for example, the car you're driving is understeering slightly in slow corners and you want it to oversteer, think about how you can alter your driving style to help the situation. What normally happens is you get a little frustrated with the understeer and try to force the car to go faster. About all that does is make the understeer worse, slowing you even more. Usually, you're better off being patient with an understeering car. Slow down a little more on the entrance to the turn—working the weight transfer to your advantage—and concentrate on getting good acceleration out of the corner onto the straight.

What I'm saying is, when the car is not handling the way you would like, think it through. Think about whether there is a way you can modify your driving style to suit the car. It may be easier and less expensive than trying to modify and adjust the car.

Driving Style versus Handling Problems

Your driving style or technique may actually be the cause of what you consider to be a handling problem. So, whenever you are having a handling problem with your car, don't just think about how to adjust or modify the car's suspension and aerodynamics. Consider your driving style—or perhaps driving errors. The first thing to determine when dealing with a handling problem is whether you are causing the problem. Take a real good look at your driving style and be honest. You influence the weight transfer and tire traction at each corner of the car, and at each and every turn on the track, in a variety of ways. If you are too hard on the throttle in the middle of a turn (probably because your corner entry speed was too low, and now you're trying to make up for it by accelerating too hard), you may cause

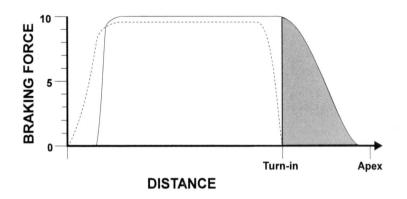

If you graphed the perfect brake force application, it would look like the solid line in the graph above. The shaded area is the trail braking phase. The dotted line shows three common braking errors. First, the initial application of the brakes is too soon and too slow. Second, the driver is not using all of the brake force available—it's just under 10. And last—and probably the worst thing—the driver finishes braking too soon. By not keeping the front of the car loaded by trail braking, the car would probably understeer beginning right at the turn-in point. Is that a chassis setup problem or a driving style problem?

the car to either understeer or oversteer. How and when you use any of the controls can often cause—or cure—a perceived handling problem.

For example, when entering a turn, if you turn the steering into the corner too quickly—not giving the front tires a chance to build up their traction forces gradually—you may experience an initial turn-in understeer. This is particularly true if you do not trail-brake enough.Is this initial understeer a handling problem—something for which you should modify the chassis setup? Or are you turning too gradually, never getting the car to take a set in the corner until you're halfway through it?

Sure, you should work on adjusting the suspension to help cure any problem. But by doing that you may cause another problem elsewhere (such as an oversteer during the midcorner or exit). Instead, it may be better to adjust or improve your driving style or technique. The key is analyzing and recognizing the problem.

Now, don't get me wrong. I don't suggest trying to overcome every handling problem by altering your driving. Always consider how you can improve the car. But don't fool yourself. Look at your driving technique as well.

Chapter 19

Practicing and Testing

Your mental approach to testing and practice is important. You want to simulate the competitive spirit and environment as closely as possible. You want the same intensity and aggressiveness in practice as you show in the race. If you practice at 99 percent, that's how you will perform in the race. It's very difficult to get back up to 100 percent.

SPEED SECRET #28:
Practice how you plan to race, and then you'll race as you practiced.

Practice programs your mind so under actual race conditions, you instinctively respond. Treat practice and the race with the same respect and intensity. Then, during a race, you will be as relaxed and calm as if you were practicing.

There is no point in ever going on a race track if you're not going to drive at 100 percent. If you're testing or driving an endurance race where you may not want to drive right at the limit, you should still be 100 percent focused, have 100 percent concentration. There is no reason ever to think that a sloppy turn-in is good enough. You don't want to make good enough a habit. The only way to ensure that doesn't happen is always to drive at 100 percent.

We often believe the more we practice a skill or technique—over and over again, many times—the better we'll get. This is not necessarily true. Experience is not always all that it's cracked up to be. In fact, every time you practice a technique incorrectly, you're increasing your chances of doing it wrong again. It's easy to become very experienced at repeating the same mistakes.

SPEED SECRET #29:
Practice doesn't make perfect;
only perfect practice makes perfect.

So, don't practice too much at first, or you're likely to develop incorrect patterns or movements. Instead, begin with a few laps, maintaining intense concentration and motivation. Continue practicing only while concentration and interest are strong. If you begin to repeat an error, or if your concentration or attention starts to fade, if you start to become casual, then stop. Clear your head, get your concentration and motivation back, then go again.

A driver can practice many of the techniques required to win while driving on the street. Practice smooth, consistent braking, squeezing and easing the throttle, arcing the steering into and out of a turn, picking the Ideal Line through a corner, being smooth, and keeping the car balanced.

You don't have to drive fast to do this. This is not just physical practice. Just as a golfer or tennis player "grooves" his swing, you are "grooving" your car-control techniques. Each time you apply the brakes or turn the steering wheel, your actions are being programmed into your brain. The more your technique is programmed, the easier, smoother, and more natural it will be in the heat of the battle on the track.

A lot of race drivers practice bad habits when driving on the street. They don't hold the steering wheel properly, they rest their hand on the shifter, they don't squeeze the brake and gas pedals, and so on. How do they expect to drive any differently at speed on the race track when they've just programmed those techniques into their heads? And if you can't do something at slow speed on the street, you'll never be able to do it naturally on the race track. It's the same with any sport. What do you think would happen if Andre Agassi practiced hitting one-handed backhands all year, and then went to Wimbledon and played using a two-handed backhand?

One of your objectives during practice is finding the right chassis setup for the race and/or qualifying. For the race, you want a comfortable, consistent, reliable setup. For qualifying, you may want a setup that is less "comfortable"—perhaps with less aerodynamic downforce—but is fast for one or two laps. A good race setup allows you to know you can move up from where you qualified.

The first few laps of a practice session may be the time to bed in new brake pads or scrub in a new set of tires. Generally, with most brake pads, the trick is to heat them up gradually by braking heavily (but be careful as they can begin to fade at anytime—so brake hard, but early), and then run a few easy laps to let them cool. Since this is not always the best procedure for bedding pads—and some come prebedded—check with the manufacturer first.

Concentrate on the car's setup and what you can do to improve it. Part of your job is to become sensitive to what the car is doing.

Check the brake bias by overbraking at different locations to see if the front or rear tires lock up first. How is the handling in the slow corners? The medium-speed corners? The fast corners? How is the initial turn-in? Does it understeer or oversteer? What about the middle of the corner? Does it put the power down well on the exit of the corner, or is there too much wheelspin? Does the car bottom out going over bumps, or can you get away with lowering it? Does the car feel too soft—does it roll and pitch too much in the turns? Is it too stiff—does it feel like it's "skating" across the track with too little grip? Are the shocks too soft, too stiff? What are the effects of an antiroll bar sweep (see "antiroll bar" in chapter 4)?

How are the gear ratios? What is the maximum rpm on the longest straight? Are there corners where having a slightly taller or lower gear ratio would help?

Consider how each change interrelates. That is, if you change the handling to better suit one particular corner, will the gear ratio still be correct, or will it be too low with the extra speed you're carrying? Consider the top gear ratio—what about in a draft? Will it be too low a gear when you pick up a few extra miles per hour in the draft?

Obviously, you can't do much of this setup development until you know the track well. If you're making improvements each lap in your driving, how are you going to know if a change you made to the car helped or not? This is where consistency comes in.

At the same time, practice is where you should try different things. Try taking a corner in a taller gear. Try braking later and carrying more speed into a turn. Or the opposite—brake earlier and work on getting on the power earlier in the turn. Which works best? Follow a quicker car, noticing when it brakes and how it takes the corners.

Debrief with your engineer, mechanic, or just yourself after each session. Make notes on everything about the car and your driving.

The real question you need to ask yourself is this: "What can I do to go faster?"

One final comment about practice. It's dumb to crash in practice. Practicing is for learning the track and finding the right setup for the car so you will be quick in qualifying and in the race. Don't waste it by crashing. There isn't much satisfaction in having someone say, "It's a shame about that crash—you almost won that practice session!"

Chapter 20

Qualifying

Obviously, it's important to qualify well. The closer to the front of the grid you are, the fewer cars you have to pass. Plus, psychologically, it gives you an edge on everyone you outqualified.

Qualifying can be an art in itself. Being able to pull off one extremely quick lap is what it's all about.

If you're qualifying during a group-qualification session, as is the case in most roadracing events, it's often best to wait for a clear gap in traffic. There is not much point in driving among a group of cars, only to have them slow you down. Sometimes you concentrate more on "racing" the cars around you, rather than focusing on what you need to do.

Having said that, some drivers actually perform best when there is a little extra incentive—like chasing another car. Plus, you may be able to get a good draft off the car in front. But be careful you don't get too caught up in what the competition is doing. Again, focus on your own performance.

As I said earlier, you may want to set up the car a little differently for qualifying. Sometimes setting the car up a little looser (so it oversteers more) or with less downforce is best for a couple of quick laps, but would be very difficult to control for the entire length of a race.

There also comes a time in qualifying when you may have to go for what former World Champion Niki Lauda called a "chaotic lap." This is where you push for that last extra tenth or hundredth of a second. This may mean leaving your braking that fraction longer, entering a turn a fraction quicker, or taking that almost flat-out corner absolutely flat-out. Obviously, this can be the most dangerous driving you ever do. It will likely be the most thrilling as well—and the most satisfying when it all works out.

Qualifying for an oval track race, where one car at a time makes a qualifying run, is probably the most pressure-filled moment of your life. But like anything, the more experience you have doing it, the easier it gets.

I'd say the keys to single car qualifying on an oval are:

• Spin the rear tires while leaving the pit lane to heat them up a bit.

• To heat up the front tires, make the car understeer by quickly turning in lots of steering angle while accelerating as you drive into turns one and two of the oval (be careful, though, because when the front tires get grip it is easy to spin the car).

• It's critical to get up to speed as quickly as possible, so accelerate hard. Use all the engine rpm.

- If it is a track where you need to brake (some ovals are flat-out all the way around), drag the brakes with your left foot all the way down the back straight on the warm-up lap.

- Weave back and forth as much as possible down the back straight on your warm-up lap.

- Drive through turns three and four as quickly as possible to get momentum for your first lap.

- In some series, your first lap past the start/finish line will be the first timed lap, while in other series it is the second pass. Either way, concentrate on your exit speed out of turn four as you approach the start of your first lap.

It's important to be very focused for qualifying, whether it's by yourself on an oval or in a pack on a roadracing circuit. This is where you really have to shut out everything else around you and visualize yourself driving perfectly on the track, pushing for that very last ounce of speed. Then, once you're on the track, just let it flow—don't "try." If you're focused and you've visualized what you want to do, it should come naturally. Let it happen.

At Sebring in 1995, I drove for Craig T. Nelson and his Screaming Eagles IMSA World Sports Car team. We had a number of engine problems during practice, blowing one up in the last practice just before qualifying. The crew made a quick engine change to get ready for qualifying, but the throttle setup was a little different on the new engine. The result was a throttle pedal that worked like an on-off switch—there was no way of modulating the pedal. Literally, it was like turning the ignition switch off and on.

The crew worked as hard as they could to make it right before the qualifying session began, but we ran out of time. With 10 minutes already gone out of a 20-minute session, I went out to qualify. I had been sitting in the car while the crew worked on it, noticing that the throttle would stick to the floor just a little.

But now it was time to qualify. Nothing else mattered. It didn't matter how bad the car was, I was going to have to work around it. What mattered was being able to block out the problems—be aware of them, but not bothered by them—and the fact that I had only a few laps to set a decent time.

The key was to focus only on what mattered—going quick—and not on what didn't matter—the problems. I really had to shut out everything. But you can't not think about something. All you can do is think about, or focus, on what is important.

So, as the crew worked on the car, I kept visualizing every last detail of how I was going to drive my qualifying lap. I focused on what I was going to do, and that automatically blocked out the problems. And it worked. We qualified sixth overall, more than one second quicker than we had gone in practice.

Chapter 21

The Race

Before a race, think about where you are starting on the grid. Who is starting around you and what are they like to race with? Can you trust them running wheel-to-wheel? Are they fast starters? Do they run a few fast laps, then begin to fade? Analyze those factors and have a plan before you head out for the start of the race.

During your first pace lap (or the first lap of a practice or qualifying session for that matter), your first priority is to get the tires and brakes up to operating temperature. Many drivers will weave back and forth across the track to heat the tires. This is great, but be careful. Often, you will end up in the "marbles" off-line. Many drivers have spun out doing this. Also, drivers can get so caught up trying to warm their tires, they actually collide. Pay attention to what the other drivers around you are doing. Don't be surprised by someone accelerating and then braking very hard.

In fact, race tires will heat up quicker from hard acceleration and braking than just weaving back and forth from side to side. On pace laps, I like to weave back and forth to heat up the tires, while heating up the brakes with my left foot. I'll also accelerate hard in a straight line (getting some wheelspin), and then brake heavily. If possible, I'll hang back a little when approaching a corner, then accelerate to take the turn quickly—even trying to work the steering wheel back and forth to scrub the front tires. At the same time, I'm taking one last good look at the track surface, in case some oil or anything else spilled on it in the previous races. If it's raining, I really work the car around to feel how slippery it is. I want to make sure I'm comfortable with what the car is going to feel like during the opening laps.

At the start, look far ahead, not just at the cars around you. If possible, watch the start of other races to see where (approximately) the starter drops the green flag. And if you are using a two-way radio, have a pit crew member watch the starter and radio you as soon as he sees the flag drop.

Sometimes you can hang back just a little from your grid position, then begin to accelerate just slightly before you think the green flag is going to drop. If you've timed it right you will have a slight advantage on the others around you. If not, you will have to ease off the throttle. What you don't want is for the flag to drop just as you're backing off the gas.

In fact, depending on your grid position, once you have started to accelerate, don't lift. If you do and the green flag drops, you are going to lose positions. If you try to anticipate the green and begin accelerating, stay on it (within reason, obviously). If you do this, one of two things will occur:

- The flag drops just after you begin to accelerate and you get a jump on the field, or
- The starter doesn't drop the green flag and there will be a second pace lap (don't try jumping the start the second time).

Be careful going into the first turn on the first lap, as more crashes occur here than any-where else. Having said that, it is very important to get a good start. If you start too conserv-atively and lose contact with the lead pack of cars, you may never be able to make up for it.

SPEED SECRET #30:
Races are not won in the first corner; however, they are often lost there.

It's usually best to run as quick as you can for the first few laps, then settle into a comfortable, consistent pace—all the while ready to take advantage of any opportunity to pass. Never turn down an opportunity to pass—you may not get it again.

SPEED SECRET #31:
Most races are decided in the last 10 percent of the race.

Be sure you're able to run strong at the end. Sometimes that means saving the car for the end of the race, being a little easy on the brakes, tires, or whatever.

Never give up, no matter how far behind you are, no matter how unlikely it seems you will catch your competitor in front of you. Keep pushing until the checkered flag falls. You never know if the competition is having problems that might be terminal if they have to dri-ve hard to fend you off. How many times have you seen the leader of a race have a me-chanical problem with only a few laps to go? You will never be able to take advantage of their problems if you are not close.

SPEED SECRET #32:
You have to be close to take advantage of luck.

The most successful racers of all time, people such as Jackie Stewart, Alain Prost, Al Unser, Rick Mears, Richard Petty, and Dale Earnhardt all have one thing in common—they finish races. In fact, if you look closely they have an incredible finishing record. Never forget, "To finish first, first you have to finish."

Most of these drivers would also agree that you should attempt to win at the slow-est speed possible. Some drivers are not content just to win the race. They feel they have to set lap records every lap, or lap the entire field. Most of these drivers have a poor fin-ishing record. They also have a poor winning record. All anyone remembers is who won. It doesn't matter by how much you win, just that you win.

Experience, practice, and a little thought—not to mention a well-prepared crew—are the keys to successful pit stops. Simply put, as a driver your job is to stop the car right on the exact marks set by your crew, stay calm while you're stopped, perform whatever functions your team requires (reset the fuel counter, foot on or off brakes, etc.), and be ready to go the second the crew is finished. Be sure you know exactly what is expected of you by your team during a pit stop.

Seeing your pit while speeding down pit lane and determining exactly where to stop can be a challenge at some tracks. Know what kind of signal your crew is going to give you, as well as having some other form of reference point for your pit (the exact number of pits past the pit lane entrance or from the end, in relation to the start/finish line, etc.).

One aspect of pit stops often overlooked is your "in" and "out" laps. Many drivers click into pit stop mode (mentally stopped) on the entire lap before entering the pit lane. They then take forever to get back up to race speed after the stop. Instead, you want to drive flat-out until the very last second before diving into pit lane, then return to the track as quickly as possible (remembering you may be on cold tires). Watch an Indy car race and make note of how little time Michael Andretti spends on his in and out laps compared to other drivers—and how much he gains on them during that time.

Endurance Races

Races of at least three hours in length and requiring a driver change are usually considered endurance races. Typically they are 6, 12, or 24 hours long.

It is a good idea for any driver to compete in as many endurance races as possible, no matter what type of car it's in. In terms of seat time, you can't beat it. You will often drive for at least 1 1/2-hour stints and perhaps up to 3 hours. It's great practice and really trains you to concentrate for a long period of time. This is going to help a lot when competing in sprint races. Plus, you learn to "save" the car—not to abuse it mechanically. This practice will rub off on your sprint race driving technique.

In most endurance races, many classes of cars will be competing which means you will get a lot of practice passing and being passed—perhaps as much in one race as you would in an entire season of a one-class or "spec" series.

When driving endurance races, it's important to get yourself into a rhythm early and stick to the pace you and the team have decided on. Avoid getting caught up in a heavy battle with another car. Yes, you want to beat your competitors, but pace yourself. Sometimes, if you can't pass and pull away from a competitor, you're better off following them for a while. Often this will result in them losing concentration and making a mistake.

Obviously, in an endurance race, pit stops are going to play a vital role. Make sure your team practices them. And practice driver changes. Often, the amount of time spent in the pits fueling and changing drivers determines the outcome of the race.

Driver changes can be difficult. The biggest problem is the varying sizes of drivers. Seating position and comfort are sometimes a compromise. But remember that the seating position will affect your performance, and do everything possible to minimize the compromises.

A general rule in endurance racing is this: The less time spent in the pits, the better your chances of winning. I know this sounds obvious, but it's surprising how many teams seem to ignore this, and instead rely on their speed on the track. Nothing is more frustrating than beating a competitor on the track, only to have them beat you overall through better pit work and strategy. Besides, it's much less expensive to improve a team's pit work speed than to improve the car's speed.

Chapter 22

Driver as Athlete

Is a race driver an athlete? This question has been knocked around for years. Who cares? All I know is it takes great physical skill and endurance to drive a race car well, not to mention the extreme mental demands.

If you want to be even the slightest bit successful in racing, you need to be in good physical condition. If you want to win, if you want to make racing your profession, then you must be in very good condition.

Driving a race car requires aerobic fitness, muscle strength and flexibility, and proper nutritional habits. Without these you will be lacking in the strength and endurance not only to be successful, but also to race safely. Using the controls (steering, brakes, throttle, clutch, shifter) and dealing with the tremendous g-forces on your body demand a great deal more than most people think, especially with the extreme heat in which you usually have to work.

To qualify for your racing license, and every year or two after that (depending on the level of license you have), you must have a full physical test completed by your doctor. But even though you may be healthy according to a doctor, how physically fit are you? How strong? How supple and flexible?

When your body tires during a race, it not only affects your physical abilities, but also your mental abilities. When you physically tire, and you begin to notice aches and pains (and even before you notice them), it distracts your mind from what it should be doing—concentrating on driving as quickly as possible.

The better conditioned your body is, the more mentally alert you will be and able to effectively deal with the stress and concentration levels. A big part of the drain on your strength is the very intense and never-ending concentration you must maintain. Just a slight lapse in concentration can bring disaster. How many times have you heard the expression "brain fade" used as an excuse?

Notice how often a driver's lap times begin to progressively slow near the end of a race. The driver usually blames it on the tires going off, the brakes fading, or the engine losing power. If the truth be known, it's usually the driver that's going off, fading, or losing power as fatigue sets in.

Drivers who claim to stay in shape simply by racing are only fooling themselves. The workout you get from racing even every weekend is not good enough. You must supplement that with a regular physical conditioning program.

Physical Conditioning

When you train, you become more fit. Stressing your body, in a controlled manner, through running, lifting weights, or whatever exercise you choose gradually breaks down the muscle fiber. Then, with rest, the muscles heal stronger. So each time you exercise, then rest, your body becomes stronger.

Use a regular fitness training program to improve your coordination, strength, flexibility, and endurance. Sports like running, tennis, racquetball, and squash are excellent for improving your cardiovascular fitness and coordination. Added to a specially designed weight training and stretching program, these activities may mean the difference between winning and losing. Most of these will also improve your reaction skills as well.

Strength, particularly in a modern ground-effects car, is very important, so weight training is a key. Keep in mind though, you don't want to bulk up too much if driving formula-type cars, as the cockpits tend to be very cramped. Concentrate on building muscle endurance as much as outright strength.

In 1985 and 1986 I drove a Trans-Am car. We were a relatively low-budget team, especially in comparison with the factory teams. At the time, power-assisted steering had just begun to be used. Driving one of those cars without power steering was a real workout. It took so much physical effort to steer them. Eventually, we put power steering in our car. I couldn't believe the difference. Not just in my fatigue level, though. I could now drive faster. In fact, without doing anything else to the car we improved our lap times by close to a second. The difference was I was able to drive consistently at the limit. I hadn't realized how much I had kept in reserve before, particularly in fast corners with the odd bump. If I hit a bump at the limit, I probably wouldn't have been able to hold onto the steering wheel—it would have been pulled out of my grip. With power steering, I could consistently drive at the limit without that worry. Plus, I could "throw" the car into a turn, feeling confident I could turn the wheel quick enough to catch it. This experience really made me realize how important strength is to driving. And I know I became a faster Indy car driver when I improved my strength level.

You now understand how critical it is to be sensitive to what the car is telling you, and how important it is to be precise in your use of the controls. Try this test: Trace over a picture with a pencil—very accurately and with great detail. Then do 50 push-ups. Try tracing the picture again. What happened? When the muscles in your arms tire, you lose some of the precise control. You need that precise control when driving a race car.

Your cardiovascular system takes a real workout when racing. The average person's heart rate at rest is between 50 and 80 beats per minute (bpm)—less than half its maximum potential. Most athletes operate during their sport at around 60 to 70 percent of their maximum, and then often only for a few minutes at a time between rests. Studies have shown race drivers at any level often operate at close to 80 percent of their maximum bpm—for the entire length of the race.

Being aerobically fit, then, will make the difference between winning and losing. The only way to ensure your cardiovascular system is in shape is through aerobic training: running, cycling, Stairmaster, etc.—any sport where you keep your heart rate at 60 to 70 percent of its maximum for at least 20 minutes, and preferably more.

Your reflexes can be developed. Sports such as squash, racquetball, and table tennis are great for improving your hand-eye coordination and reflexes. Computer and video games are also good for improving your mental processing and reflexes.

It's only been over the last few years that I've really begun to realize the benefits of flexibility. As part of my regular training program, I now spend quite some time stretching—working on my flexibility. Since starting this, I've had fewer muscle aches and much less cramping while driving—and feel a lot better the day after the race.

Should you ever crash, the more flexible your body, the less chance you have of being injured. With a flexible body, your muscles will be better able to accommodate the forces from an impact.

How's your weight? If you are overweight, you owe it not only to yourself, but also to your car and team to lose weight. Why have your team work at making the car as light as possible, if you're not? But more importantly, excess fat on your body works as insulation—something you don't need in the high-heat environment of a race car cockpit. Reducing your body fat content (or maintaining it if you're already lean enough) should be a part of your training program.

In fact, heat is one of the race driver's worst enemies. The combination of all the fire-resistant clothing, the continuous physical exertion, and the heat generated by many race cars makes for a less-than-ideal working environment. A driver's body temperature can reach over 100 degrees.

This heat often leads to dehydration. Some drivers will lose up to 5 percent of their body weight in perspiration during a race. This can lead to weakened and cramping muscles, and less-effective mental processing. In fact, studies have shown that losing just 2 percent of your body weight in sweat can reduce your work capacity by as much as 15 percent. There is only one solution for dehydration: drink fluids. Over the course of a race weekend, especially in warm weather, try to take in as much water as possible—at least four quarts or liters per day on race weekends.

During the Sebring 12-Hour IMSA race in 1994, I became very dehydrated. It was a really hot day, and my co-driver had problems, which meant I had to drive close to four of the first five hours. When I drank fluid from the drink bottle in the car, it made me sick to my stomach. By about nine hours into the race I was so dehydrated that I became very weak and dizzy. We ended up having to get a relief driver for the last hour, while I spent time in the medical center having fluids replaced by I.V. Early in the day I had made sure I was drinking lots of fluids, but because I got sick, they didn't stay in me for long. It was a very unpleasant experience, and could have cost us positions in the race.

It is a well-known fact that an athlete's diet is extremely important to his or her performance. Marathon runners are famous for their carbo-loading (eating very high-carbohydrate foods) prior to races. A race driver is no different. Again, if you want to win, follow a proper diet. Talk to a doctor or nutritionist. At the very least, avoid foods with high fat content on race weekends. Stick to high-carbohydrate meals.

Finally, do you drink much? How about smoking? We all know that alcohol and cigarettes affect your health. Even if there is a one-in-a-million chance that they could slow your reactions, affect your vision, or decrease your cardiovascular level, consider whether you want to take that chance. How committed are you to being successful?

The effects of alcohol on your body and mind can last for a long time. It slows your reaction time, dulls your senses, and slows your ability to make decisions. And taking drugs to improve your performance is a major mistake. Not only will it not help, it's very dangerous.

SPEED SECRET #33:
Given equal cars and equal talent, the driver who is in the best physical condition is going to win.

Often a driver with less talent and less car will win due to his fitness level. So if you want to race, if you want to win, you owe it to yourself to be as physically fit as possible.

Chapter 23

Winning

The final chapter in this part on the mental and physical techniques you need to be successful is about the ultimate goal—winning.

Sometimes a driver has to learn how to win. Often, it takes a win—whether it be a total fluke or a deserved win—for a driver (and team) to learn that they can win and believe they can win. Once that happens, a driver often gets on a roll and the victories just seem to happen.

I don't know how many times I've seen a driver and team who have everything it takes to win but who can't seem to do it. Then, after almost fluking out a win, watch out. All of a sudden, you can't stop them. They start winning everything in sight.

That's why I feel it's important for a driver to race where he or she can win. If you're racing in a very competitive series where you can't seem to pull off a win, don't be afraid to go back and do a race or two in a lesser or easier series just to practice winning. Then take that winning attitude back to your main focus.

One of my favorite quotes is by Henry Ford. He said, "If you think you can, or think you can't, you're probably right." You must have total confidence in yourself and the people on your team to be a winner.

PART 4

The Finish Line

The final part of this book covers a couple of very important ingredients that don't fall into the Car/Track/Driver categories and yet contribute immensely to a successful career in racing. As I mentioned at the beginning of this book, it takes much more than just being a fast driver. Your "marketability" as a driver, sponsorship, career steps, and professionalism—the business side of racing—all play critical roles in your career. We'll take a brief look at how to manage these business elements.

The second, and perhaps the most important factor of all, is safety. It goes without saying that if you don't take safety seriously, you won't have a long and successful career.

Chapter 24

The Business of Racing

Racing today is much different from 20 or even 10 years ago. It used to be that at the professional level of the sport, a person was chosen to drive for a team strictly on talent level. Not so anymore. There are many drivers today who have the talent to win races. So when a team is looking for a driver, why not select one who is promotable and marketable—a public relations person's dream—and one who can bring sponsorship dollars to the team, as well as talent?

As much as this may seem unfair, it is a fact you will have to live with during your career. You can either choose to make the most of it—look at it as an extra challenge—or be miserable because you're not getting your "breaks."

You can't sit back and wait for a team to come to you, thinking that because you're a good driver you deserve it. The days of car owners coming to knock on your door are few and far between. These days, if you want a ride, you have to go after it yourself. And probably bring something to the table, as well.

I'm not saying that you will have to pay for your racing throughout your career. Even today, some drivers are selected to drive for a top team based primarily on their talent. But even they had to pay their dues. They probably had to bring personal or sponsorship money to the teams they drove for on the way to the top.

Don't ever look at this as being beneath you. If you don't believe sponsorship, professionalism, and public relations are important to your career, you'll be watching a lot of racing on television.

Danny Sullivan has this to say, "The one area the modern-day race car driver needs to focus on that may be the most important part on the road to success in this sport is the raising of sponsorship. Very few drivers who I have met over the years are wealthy enough to fund the way to the top. Sure, there are a lot of people who can pay for a season in Formula Ford or Atlantic, but at some stage of your career you need sponsorship. The most frequently asked question to me is, 'How do I get started in racing if I don't have any money?' Unlike other sports where you need a pair of shoes, a racquet, or ball and a place to play, racing requires expensive cars, tires, fuels, rebuilds, and an expensive place to run them. All of this and on an ongoing basis takes serious money."

Career Moves

As I've said before, it takes a lot more than just driving skill to be successful in racing. You must have all the right components of "the program" to be a consistent winner. Components like the right equipment (car, spares, etc.), a good crew (mechanics, engineers, team manager, etc.—even if one person handles many of these jobs on a small team), an adequate budget (adequate being a relative term), an appropriate testing program, and more. Then all these components have to mesh together. It's especially important that the people work together as a team. Without that, no matter how good you are, you won't win on a regular basis.

Many drivers aren't interested in trying to climb to the top of professional racing. They just want to race for fun in amateur events. Nothing wrong with that. I know many people who have been amateur racers for years and love it for the thrill of competition, the sense of self-satisfaction, the camaraderie and friendships developed, relaxation, and so much more.

Personally, I find racing to be the most relaxing thing in the world. When I'm racing, nothing else matters. I don't care what else is happening in my life, I'm focused on racing. It allows me to forget everything else—I just relax and enjoy my driving. And, for that reason, the level of the sport you race at is not important.

No matter what level of the sport you're involved in, however, it's going to take a lot of work. As far as I'm concerned it's worth every bit of it, every time I get behind the wheel. Having said that, to make it in professional racing takes much more work than amateur racing does. That's something to be aware of. If you're having a tough time managing the time and effort in amateur racing, don't think it's going to get any easier when you start racing in a professional series.

If you do aspire to reach the top of professional racing, the road you take to get there can vary dramatically. It differs from driver to driver. However, there are usually some common threads. It's often determined somewhat by where you live (and whether you're willing to move), your personal financial position, how good you are at raising money (sponsorship, donations, etc.), your professional approach (whether a professional team is going to want you to drive for them), and what your ultimate goal in racing is (Formula One, Indy car, NASCAR, Sports Cars, Showroom Stock, etc.). Talk to drivers who have made it. Read biographies of the great drivers. Learn what has worked for others.

PacWest CART Champ car team owner Bruce McCaw has this to say, "The first perspective drivers must realize is that it is a business, and that teamwork is vital to success. Over the long term, few drivers succeed if they don't develop the respect and support of the mechanics, pit crews, engineers, public relations and support personnel, as well as the owners, officials, and their fellow drivers. Within CART and Indy Lights, with thankfully few exceptions, one will find a really good group of dedicated and talented professionals who really care about what they are doing. The few others will usually bounce around for a while before either languishing in the periphery or simply disappearing.

"When we watch prospective or younger drivers as they develop, it is imperative that they be able to function in a team environment. Top level driving skills must be virtually a given. A driver must have a balance of technical knowledge, interpersonal skills, ambition, talent, and judgment.

"Nothing is static in this business, and one must be driven to constant learning and development. Never believe that you know it all or that you are better than everyone else. And never be afraid to admit to a mistake."

It used to be that roadracers were roadracers, oval track racers were oval track racers, and they never crossed paths. But with CART Champ cars running both road courses and oval tracks, many racing series have followed suit. Today, if you don't have experience on both types of tracks, your chances of being very successful in the top ranks of racing are reduced.

Look for opportunities to race on all types of tracks. Consider that when deciding which series in which to compete. If a series combines both oval track and road courses, and it's your goal to move up the professional racing ladder, choose that series over one racing only on one type of track. It will pay off in the long run.

If you are lucky, you'll have to make the decision between buying your own race car and renting one from a professional race car rental business or racing school. I say lucky because many drivers cannot afford the second option, and are forced to buy, manage, and maintain their own cars. There are advantages and disadvantages to both options.

First, I believe it is best to work on your own car at least for part of your career. This helps teach you many of the basic technical aspects, and makes you more mechanically sensitive to your car. In other words, you will probably learn to be a little easier on the car. The disadvantage is that you can spend so much time and concentration on the car that you may spend very little on your driving.

If you rent a race car from a professional race car rental business, it allows you to focus all your attention on your driving, leaving the mechanical worries to someone else—someone who is supposed to be better than you at looking after those details. But, beware: there are good car rental businesses and bad ones. Do your homework before choosing one. Talk to others who have used them.

Assuming you find a good rental program that allows you to devote all your concentration to your driving, don't forget the mechanical side. Being mechanically sensitive, being able to interpret what the car is doing and communicate it to your engineer or mechanic may make the difference in whether you land a ride with a top professional team.

Choosing to compete in one of the racing school series is probably the best choice strictly from a driving perspective. They usually have instructors working as coaches during race events, which will greatly speed up your learning curve. And usually they are "spec" series, where everyone is in the same type of car. This is a very good way of gauging yourself and your progress against others.

But again, be careful. There are good school series and bad ones. Some racing schools are only interested in your pocketbook. Again, do your homework. Talk with people who have raced in the series in the past.

Choosing between racing open-wheel (formula-type) or closed-wheel (production-based or sports racing) cars should be a decision based on where you want to go in the sport. If you are certain about only racing closed-wheel cars in your career, then stick with them. But, if you're not sure where your career is going to go, spend time racing open-wheel cars. If you only have experience in closed-wheel cars, it is more difficult to make the jump into an open-wheel car should the opportunity arise. Experience in open-wheel cars makes it easier to handle any type of car.

If you want a career as a professional driver, my advice is to drive every type of car you can get your hands on. Every car, from the slowest showroom stock car to the most sophisticated formula car, will teach you something different. The more you learn, the more adaptable you will be, and the more successful you will be.

A good education is also important to a driver's career. Although an engineering degree will help with the technical side of racing, I believe a strong business and marketing education is perhaps more important today. With a little effort, you can learn enough of the engineering side. Today's race drivers' success depends more on their business and marketing knowledge.

Bruce McCaw says, "As a driver, make sure you understand the big picture. Have a plan that you have thought about, both long term and short term, and most importantly, every weekend. When your plan isn't working, move to an alternative before it becomes too late. Timely decision making is critical. Be extremely careful about signing agreements with people you don't know who wish to represent you. If they have a story that sounds like a dream career, it probably is just a dream that may become a nightmare.

"Also, control your own destiny. Beware of consultants and expert managers. Seek good advice from people who you trust that have good common sense and are looking after your best interest. Always understand the issues in your driver agreements, and make sure you understand why the team or owner may have certain needs."

To reach the top in racing, you're going to have to sacrifice—a lot! Ask yourself, "Am I willing to give up everything to reach the top?" Are you willing to sell your street car? Your stereo? Give up your girlfriend or wife? (I'm not suggesting this is mandatory, but it has happened because of racing.)

If not, be truthful with yourself. Determine how much you are willing to sacrifice, and realize how far that will allow you to go. There is absolutely nothing wrong with amateur racing for fun—as long as you don't fool yourself into thinking you're going to be the next world champion without sacrifice and commitment.

You have to be 100 percent totally committed if you really want to make it to the top. You will have to commit time—24 hours a day, 7 days a week—and money, usually everything you've got for a long time.

I believe anyone can be successful in racing—maybe not a superstar but successful nevertheless—if he or she is totally committed and dedicated to doing what it takes to become successful. It takes tremendous perseverance. Bobby Rahal was once quoted as saying it takes 10 percent talent and 90 percent perseverance to be successful in racing. He wasn't saying it doesn't take talent; it's just that perseverance is so important.

I'm a perfect example. Sure, there have been more successful drivers in the history of the sport, perhaps even racers with more talent. But I've proven you can make it to the top with hard work, perseverance, determination, sacrifice, knowledge . . . and maybe just a little talent.

However, enjoy racing for what it is—and for whatever level you're at. You don't have to make the world championship your goal. Just do your best, and if things work, you'll make it. If not, step back to amateur racing and have fun. Keep your options open.

Danny Sullivan adds, "Motor racing is a passionate sport, not for the faint of heart. You have to be dedicated, focused, and driven (no pun intended!). Even with all that, you still need money."

Sponsorship

Sponsorship is what makes auto racing work. An entire book could, and has, been devoted to sponsorship (the best one I've seen is "Sponsorship and the World of Motor Racing" by Guy Edwards). So, I'm only going to touch on a few key points based on my experience.

Bruce McCaw says, "Today, the commercial side is as important as the racing side, and it is important to understand both the organization of one's team and the needs of one's sponsors. Too often the needs of sponsors are not fully understood or supported. It is hard to develop sponsors and very easy to lose them, and one bad experience with a driver has soured many a sponsor in motorsport. The dynamics of motor racing have proven to provide very successful and effective results for sponsors, but everyone has to be dedicated to making it a positive experience for them as well. This is a very small community."

The first rule of sponsorship hunting: It's not what you know, it's who you know. Ninety percent of selling a sponsorship is just getting to the decision-maker. Concentrate on meeting the right people. In every successful sponsor company, there is at least one key person who can see the benefits and will help push it through. You need to find that person. Talk to people you know to find out who they know.

If that was rule number one, then the following is rule 1 1/2: It doesn't matter what you want, what counts is what the company you're approaching wants. Too many people in racing go in to a potential sponsor and tell them what they will do if the company gives them money. Then they wonder why the company said no. Put yourself in their position. Figure out what they want and how to give it to them.

Do less talking and more listening. Find out what they want—how they can use racing to benefit them. Sometimes what they want is not necessarily what you think they need. Help them figure out what they want or need. If possible, ask them to describe to you how they envision a racing sponsorship program working for them. If they tell you, listen very carefully, because they are selling themselves. If you can supply them with their vision of the sponsorship, it's almost impossible for them to say "no." It was their idea.

The sponsor's name on the car—"the mobile billboard"—should be just the beginning of the program. Usually, what makes the program really work is the corporate entertainment at the track, the business partnership opportunities with co-sponsors, the employee morale programs, the public relations, media exposure, and so on. The sponsorship must be an overall marketing program, tied to the theme of a race car with the company's logo on it, that helps sell a product or service and builds corporate image.

It used to be that companies would sponsor a driver or car just for the exposure, image, or public relations value. That rarely cuts it anymore. If it doesn't result directly in bottom-line sales, they won't go for it.

You can spend thousands and thousands of dollars on fancy-looking presentations, brochures, and packages enthusing about how great a driver you are and how this is the best marketing program the world has ever seen. But 9 times out of 10, the person making the decision is going to decide based on you as a person, and the real core of your program. Companies buy good people with good programs—not just a good presentation.

I'm not saying you shouldn't spend money on a professional-looking presentation. You should. What I'm saying is if that's all you've got, you will have a tough time selling it. Spend time developing a good program that delivers value to a potential sponsor.

That often means using the resources of one sponsor to benefit another, and vice versa. For example, get the local newspaper to sponsor your team strictly with advertising space equal to the dollar value you require. It has cost the newspaper very little in actual dollars and in return, you give logo exposure on your car along with all the other benefits you have to give a sponsor with your program. You then offer a full sponsorship to another company, plus the newspaper advertising, in return for the budget you require. It's a win-win-win program.

You will be far better off if you target specific companies you think can benefit from a program such as yours, rather than just firing off hundreds of proposals in the mail. Take the time to do research on the company, call it, and then meet personally. Using the shotgun approach is a waste of time and money.

To sell a sponsorship, as with everything else in racing, perseverance is a must. Never give up, no matter how many "no's" you get. But don't go blindly from one "no" to another. Learn from each sales attempt. Understand why they said no, and figure out how you can avoid it in the future. In fact, selling sponsorship is a great learning experience. What you learn here will be useful in any career for the rest of your life.

You may want to use sponsor-hunting professionals. But beware. There are hundreds of so-called "professional sponsor hunters" who will waste your time, your money, and your reputation. So, check them out—get references. Talk to others who have used them.

You may not have a lot of choices of who you use to solicit sponsorships in the early stages of your career, so stay very close to their efforts. Always remember, they are selling you and your reputation, so be sure you are comfortable with how they are doing so, how they portray your reputation, and the promises they make on your behalf.

Once you have signed a sponsor, don't just take their money and go racing. Getting the sponsor is just the beginning. You, working with the sponsor, will have to exploit the sponsorship program. If not, kiss them good-bye. It just won't work for them. If it's not improving their bottom line, they won't stay involved. And to do that, they need to have more than just their name on the side of a race car. You are going to have to work very hard to give them what they want.

Danny Sullivan says, "I drove with Roger Penske from 1985 to 1991, and he had his sponsors in place. My job was not only to produce results on the track, but also to make that relationship with the sponsor, their customers, and management feel this is the place to be."

Communicate with your sponsors once you have them. What often keeps a sponsorship program going is your personal relationship with the individuals involved in making the decisions. Cultivate that, but don't be phony or try too hard. Successful business people will see right through that.

Try to progress with a sponsor. It's tough to sell a million-dollar sponsor right off the bat, but over a period of time with the opportunity to show what you can do, it's possible.

In fact, it's important to educate your sponsors. You have to show them what you and racing can do . . . for them.

Danny Sullivan says, "One of the very first people I met in racing was Jackie Stewart. I worked as a gofer for him and Tyrrell for a year. Not only was he one of the best drivers of all time, with 27 Grand Prix wins in 99 starts, he was—and is— the best with the sponsors ever. He still has some of the same sponsors since he stopped driving in 1974. Unheard of! A modern-day driver must learn the art of setting their car up, working with the engineers, driving in all conditions, on all kinds of tracks, and finding those sponsors. And more importantly, maintaining that relationship with those sponsors."

Be careful what you or your agent promise a sponsor, especially as far as your on-track results go. If you promise to win every race in sight and don't, you lose credibility and probably their support. If you promise to finish last in every race, they probably won't want to be involved. Make sure you give them realistic expectations. This also applies to the exposure and marketing results they will get from the program.

Finally, a sponsorship program must work off the track. It should be a good value to the sponsor before you and your car ever get on the track. Anything you do on the track is a bonus, especially if it's running at the front of the pack, generating that extra exposure.

Now here's my opinion on business ethics relating to sponsorship hunting: don't try to steal other drivers' or teams' sponsors. I believe that hurts everyone—it hurts the sport. If you go after a company already involved as a racing sponsor, usually all you accomplish is to demonstrate how unprofessional people can be in motorsports. Sometimes that results in the company deciding it doesn't want to stay involved in this sport. Everyone loses.

If another team's existing sponsor approaches you indicating they are dissatisfied where they are now and would be interested in hearing about what you can offer, then that's fair game. Otherwise, leave them alone. There are enough other potential sponsors out there. It's the same as driving: concentrate on your own performance rather than your competition's and you will win in the end.

Danny Sullivan says, "Let's not forget, to make those race cars go faster than the other guy's, you have to test, have the latest trick, be developing your own things, and this takes cubic dollars—sponsorship is the key."

Professionalism and Personal Image

How you are perceived by the outside world (business community, media, etc.) and the racing community can have a great effect on your career. If you want to be a professional race driver, you must look and act professional. That includes how you dress (appropriate for each occasion), your personal appearance, the way you speak, how you act in company, and so on.

Any letter or sponsorship proposal that has anything to do with you must be first-class. That will often be the first impression you make with a potential sponsor, team, or media contact. And you know what they say about first impressions.

What you do outside of the car is just as important as what you do in the car. Remember, a big part of your job as a race driver is as a motivator/team leader. You can have all the talent in the world, but if you don't have absolutely everyone around you pulling for you and helping you, you will not make it in this sport. There are many examples of talented drivers who have had their careers cut short by their actions outside the cockpit.

How you "present" yourself outside the car will play the most important role in the rides you get in the future. How you act, react, and interact with all the people around you will determine how often you win. If your actions do not motivate your mechanics, engineers, team owner, sponsors, media people, and so on, you will not get the competitive rides you need, you will lose good rides, you will lose the edge you require to win.

Always remember, if you're not doing everything possible to win, some of your competition is, and that is probably what will make them beat you, even if you have more natural talent. If you are unsportsmanlike outside the car, sponsors will stay away from you—so will team owners, mechanics, the media, and everyone else you need on your side.

Public Relations

Public relations is an integral part of modern-day racing. You can have all the talent in the world, but if no one knows about you, your career won't be a long one. Guaranteed, as good as you may be, there is someone else as good, or just about as good, who has a dynamite P.R. person and program letting the world know. If you want to compete on the track, you also have to compete off the track.

If you want sponsors to help support your racing program, you will have to learn all about media and public relations. Don't ever feel that promoting yourself is beneath you, or that the media should come to you because of how good you are. Those days are gone. These days a driver must not only be talented on the track, he or she must also be talented in the promotions business.

Using a professional public relations firm can be a benefit to your career if you can afford one. However, much like sponsor hunters, beware—look for the good ones.

I strongly recommend taking a public speaking course. If you are successful in racing and want your career to continue, you will have to make speeches at some point. Learn to make the most of the opportunity.

You will also have to do many interviews, either live on radio or TV, or with print journalists. Again, learn to make the most of these opportunities. There are courses that teach you how to be effective in getting across what you want to say in an interview, not just what the interviewer wants you to say.

Be yourself, though, in interviews and when making speeches and public appearances. Too many drivers today have become too "polished and practiced." They sound like a "canned" press release. Let your enthusiasm for the sport and your personality shine through, and you will find the media and sponsors more interested in listening to you.

Chapter 25

Communications, Data, & Records

When you are out on the track, whether in practice, qualifying, or the race itself, it's important to know certain information. Things like your lap time, position in the race or in qualifying, how far ahead or behind you are from your nearest competitors, time left in the qualifying session, and how many laps left in the race. Usually that information is relayed to you via a pit board or radio.

It's important that both you and your crew member working the pit board know what each signal means. It's critical for the board man to know what information you are going to want at various times. Discuss this beforehand.

During the race, I really don't care about my lap times. All I want to know is my position, the plus or minus on the cars behind and in front of me, when to pit, and what lap I'm on. Of course, in qualifying, all I care about is my lap time and how much time is left in the session. Personally, I like to have the board shown or some radio communication every lap, whether I have time to acknowledge it or not. I feel more in control knowing what's going on. I spend a lot of time before going out on the track making sure the guy with the pit board or on the radio knows exactly what I want.

However, there are times where I've purposely not had my lap times shown or told to me during a qualifying session. It's easy to focus too much on the time. For me, that sometimes led to either "trying" to go faster or believing a certain time was some sort of barrier. You may want to try a qualifying session without knowing your lap times; see if it works for you.

A two-way radio is probably the best way of relaying information as the driver can give input as well. However, there is often a lot of interference on the radio, so you can't always count on it. For that reason, many teams rely on the pit board, only using the radio as a backup for the basic information. The radio's most important use is for more-detailed information such as when there is a problem with the car, when to pit, or when the green flag is dropped.

It's also a good idea to have a couple of basic hand signals that your crew will understand for problems like a tire losing air, engine problem, low on fuel, and, especially, a nonfunctioning radio.

Data Acquisition

More and more teams are using data acquisition equipment. This can be invaluable once you learn how to get, and interpret, all the information from it. Many people

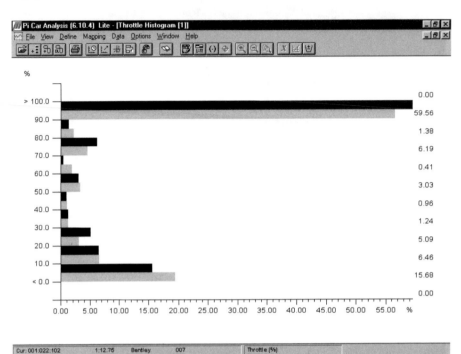

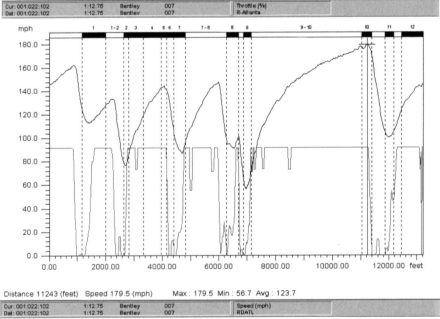

Understanding data acquisition systems is a must for drivers. The upper throttle histogram graph compares the percentage of throttle openings for two separate laps. The bottom graph shows speed and throttle position over the course of a lap.

pay a lot of money for data acquisition equipment, only to never learn how to get the most from it.

Data acquisition systems are wonderful tools for a number of reasons. First, they can tell you things about the car and your driving that you haven't noticed. They are also great at confirming what you already thought. A data acquisition system can be your "driver coach" and help you determine how to go faster. Most systems will show exactly where on the track you begin braking, your throttle position, the g-forces generated in the turns, your speed, rpm, and many engine functions. This can help you figure out where it may be possible to pick up some speed, especially if you can compare with a teammate or another driver in a similar car. And most important, they never lie. It's amazing how often you think you are taking a fast sweeper flat-out, only to have the computer show that you did ease off the throttle slightly. After every practice or qualifying session or race, I sit down and go through every detail on the computer. I know it's going to help make me faster, and if I don't use it, I'll be left behind by my competitors who do.

James Weaver says: "One of my favorite pieces of information the data acquisition system can give is a full-throttle histogram—telling me what percentage of the lap I'm at full throttle. If the percentage increases after changes to the car or driving technique, I'm bound to be faster."

Driver's Records

A driver should keep a record or log book with the details of each and every race, practice, test, or qualifying session. Learn from these records, looking back at them when returning to the same track, or when you are having a problem with a specific area of your driving.

Before each session I like to write down my objectives for that session and what driving techniques or plans I need to use to achieve them. Then, after each session, I make comments on the track and conditions, what changes were made and need to be made to the car, and what the results of the session were.

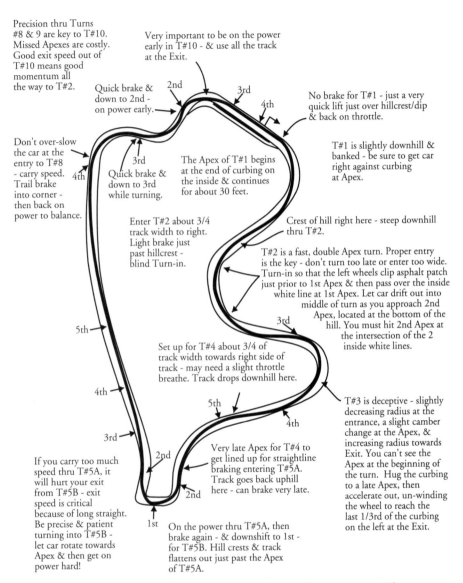

Precision thru Turns #8 & 9 are key to T#10. Missed Apexes are costly. Good exit speed out of T#10 means good momentum all the way to T#2.

Very important to be on the power early in T#10 - & use all the track at the Exit.

Quick brake & down to 2nd - on power early.

2nd

3rd

4th

No brake for T#1 - just a very quick lift just over hillcrest/dip & back on throttle.

Don't over-slow the car at the entry to T#8 - carry speed. Trail brake into corner - then back on power to balance.

3rd

4th

Quick brake & down to 3rd while turning.

The Apex of T#1 begins at the end of curbing on the inside & continues for about 30 feet.

T#1 is slightly downhill & banked - be sure to get car right against curbing at Apex.

Enter T#2 about 3/4 track width to right. Light brake just past hillcrest - blind Turn-in.

Crest of hill right here - steep downhill thru T#2.

T#2 is a fast, double Apex turn. Proper entry is the key - don't turn too late or enter too wide. Turn-in so that the left wheels clip asphalt patch just prior to 1st Apex & then pass over the inside white line at 1st Apex. Let car drift out into middle of turn as you approach 2nd Apex, located at the bottom of the hill. You must hit 2nd Apex at the intersection of the 2 inside white lines.

5th

4th

3rd

Set up for T#4 about 3/4 of track width towards right side of track - may need a slight throttle breathe. Track drops downhill here.

3rd

5th

4th

T#3 is deceptive - slightly decreasing radius at the entrance, a slight camber change at the Apex, & increasing radius towards Exit. You can't see the Apex at the beginning of the turn. Hug the curbing to a late Apex, then accelerate out, un-winding the wheel to reach the last 1/3rd of the curbing on the left at the Exit.

If you carry too much speed thru T#5A, it will hurt your exit from T#5B - exit speed is critical because of long straight. Be precise & patient turning into T#5B - let car rotate towards Apex & then get on power hard!

2nd

2nd

1st

Very late Apex for T#4 to get lined up for straightline braking entering T#5A. Track goes back uphill here - can brake very late.

On the power thru T#5A, then brake again - & downshift to 1st - for T#5B. Hill crests & track flattens out just past the Apex of T#5A.

A good habit to get into is making notes on a track map after every event. These prove to be invaluable the next time you go to a race at that track.

Chapter 26

Safety

Racing is dangerous, there's no doubt about it. But the danger can and should be controlled. Most drivers, myself included, have the attitude that injury "may happen to others, but never to me." I think you need to have this attitude to a certain extent. If you didn't, you would probably have too much fear to drive fast.

However, that's no excuse for not taking safety seriously. Over the course of a career in racing, you are bound to have at least a crash or two. How you fare in these crashes may be a matter of how much emphasis you place on the various safety equipment and systems you use.

Being safety conscious does not mean you are a "wimp." It only means you are a smart, professional driver. The more emphasis you put on your safety, the longer and more successful your racing career will be.

Take a good look at how serious the drivers in CART and Formula One are about safety. Just because you're driving a slower car does not mean it is any safer. In fact, it's often the opposite. The safety built into Champ and Formula One cars and the safety personnel at that level are superior. So if anyone has to take safety seriously, it's a driver at the beginning of his or her career.

Dr. Brock Walker says: "When crash impact does occur, three things can happen. One, the driver is injured. Two, the car is injured. And three, both are injured at the same time. The bottom line is that it's financially costly when any of the aforementioned occur. If you think about it logically, in a business sense, when you save the driver and the car, you save the most money; and proportionately, your odds for season-long success improve dramatically. With all of this in mind, let me illustrate a typical mistake by using an example.

"A few seasons ago I designed a custom cockpit for a world champion. Prior to completion of the job, the team decided that enough time had been spent on the driver's seat; they had no idea of the depth and importance of the work being undertaken, because there was a lack of attention given to the driver's medical history. In reality, they wanted to save money and they wanted to go testing. To make a long story short, the driver fractured a rib during the test because the seat was not completed. A new driver was summoned to drive. The new driver crashed and both the machine and the championship were lost. The opinion of the day was that the new driver was certainly capable under most circumstances, but in this instance he lacked the necessary degree of control. So how expensive was that seat?

"Safety is always the overriding factor. Any driver or family member that has suffered the consequences of an incidence will all tell you that they wish that more attention, preparation, and interest were given to cockpit safety issues, particularly the seat and headrest."

Safety Equipment

As I said, if you race for some time, the odds are you are going to be involved in some incident where you may get injured, either slightly or seriously. That is why you must pay attention to all safety equipment—yours and the car's.

So, the first rule is: buy the very best safety equipment you can.

SPEED SECRET #34:
If you can't afford good safety equipment, you can't afford to go racing.

A bargain-priced driving suit doesn't look like such a good deal when you're lying in a hospital badly burnt. The same thing applies to helmets. Buying a cheap helmet really is false economy. I like the saying, "if you have a cheap head, buy a cheap helmet."

After you buy the best equipment you can, take care of it. Don't drop or let your helmet sit upside down on the ground. Keep your driving suit clean—it won't be fire-resistant if it's covered in grease and dirt.

Not only will having the best equipment and taking care of it help save your life, but it is also a reflection of your attitude. If you look and act professional, you may have a better chance of acquiring sponsorship or being noticed by a professional team. Plus, you owe it to your family and friends to minimize the chances of injury.

Remove all jewelry before driving. Imagine what would happen if you were in a fire with a metal chain around your neck, metal watchband on your arm, or rings on your fingers. As the metal heats up, I don't need to tell you how much worse you will be burned, not to mention the complications it causes the doctors.

Check current regulations to ensure your equipment is up to standards. I am not going to quote the standards since they change frequently—which is fortunate, as they are constantly being upgraded.

Make sure you have spares of all your equipment. You spend too much on your racing to have a safety equipment failure or loss keep you out of action. It seems rather silly to spend tens of thousands of dollars on your race program, and then not be able to race because you lost a glove or the visor on your helmet broke.

Helmet

Helmets are meant to be used once—when your head is in it. If you drop it or bang it against something, it has now been used. Helmets are designed to absorb the energy of the impact by deforming and thereby destroying its structural strength. And even though the damage may not be visible, it should be checked by the manufacturer or replaced after an impact.

Many drivers, for emotional or superstitious reasons, become attached to their helmets and don't ever want to give them up. Not a good idea. Replace your helmet every couple of years whether it has been "used" or not. They also fatigue with age, especially the inner liner.

Helmets are made of fiberglass, Kevlar, carbon-fiber, or a combination of these materials. The Kevlar/carbon-fiber helmets are much lighter and a little more expensive. I believe the extra cost is worth it. It's not only easier on your neck over the course of a long race, but it also puts less strain on your neck in a crash.

I've had many drivers tell me that because they were driving a relatively slow car—perhaps a showroom stock car—they didn't need to spend the extra on a Kevlar/carbon-fiber helmet. Well, it doesn't matter how slow the car is, in a crash the g-forces are going to be very high. And the heavier the helmet, the more force on your neck. That may make the difference between being injured or not.

Take the time to ensure that your helmet fits perfectly. It should fit snugly, but not too tight. With the strap undone, you should not be able to rotate it on your head, side to side or forward-backwards. There should also not be any pressure points causing discomfort.

Do not paint a helmet without knowing what you're doing. Consult the helmet manufacturer. If you have to sand it, do so with only 600-grit paper—lightly. Do not sand through the manufacturer's paint/gel coat. Do not let solvent or paint get on the inner liner as this will destroy it. Do not bake dry a helmet paint job—let it air dry.

I believe a driver should wear only a full-face helmet, even in a closed car. They offer much more protection than an open-face helmet. However, if you choose an open-face, always wear eye protection. The bubble goggles are probably the best.

Helmets are tested and rated by the Snell and/or S.F.I. Foundations. The standards are upgraded every few years. The only helmets legal for use in racing are ones that have passed these tests. Check the rule book to find out the latest standard that a helmet must meet before going to buy one. You can bet you'll get a great deal on an outdated helmet, but it's not much good for anything except as a flower planter.

Driver's Suit

First of all, a driver's suit is not fireproof, it is fire-*retardant*. It is designed to resist flames and protect you from the heat of a fire long enough to allow you either to get away from the fire or for the fire to be put out. Speaking from experience, I'll tell you good suits accomplish this. I'm not so sure cheap ones do (and I'm never going to find out).

Before buying a suit, make sure it fits properly. A custom-fitted suit is best. Have your measurements taken very carefully, using the chart supplied by the suit manufacturer. And if it doesn't fit right, send it back to have it altered. A poor-fitting suit will be uncomfortable and perhaps even dangerous.

Check the rating of the suit. The S.F.I. Foundation certifies and rates driving suits, as does the F.I.A. An S.F.I. 3.2A-1 rating theoretically gives you approximately 2 seconds of protection; an S.F.I. 3.2A-5 gives you approximately 10 seconds; S.F.I. 3.2A-10 about 20 seconds (double the last number of the rating spec to give you an approximation of the number of seconds before you may be burnt).

Remember, these are only guidelines, not guarantees. And if a suit is not rated by S.F.I. or F.I.A., do you really want to buy it? How do you know how good it is? It may be available at a great price, but what price do you put on your body?

Once you have a properly fitted, high-quality suit, take care of it. Make a habit of getting changed before working on your car. A driver's suit is not meant to be your work coveralls. There is nothing worse than getting a fire-retardant suit covered in oil, grease, and fuel.

During practice for the Indianapolis 500 in 1993, a fuel regulator cracked while I was driving through turn four at over 200 miles per hour. The fuel sprayed forward into the cockpit and ignited. All of a sudden I was engulfed in a 2,200-degree methanol fire. Fortunately, I got the car stopped on the front straight and bailed out, while some crew members started putting the fire out. I was in this fire for close to 40 seconds, and yet the suit protected me perfectly. My face was burnt from the heat that radiated through the visor, and from when I tried to open the visor for a second to get some air. My neck was burnt where the fire got between where I had my balaclava tucked into my underwear. And my hands were burnt pretty badly for two reasons. First, because my gloves were so soaked with sweat—my hands were steam-burnt—and second, the gloves I was wearing didn't have a Nomex layer on the palms—it was just leather.

If I hadn't been wearing such good equipment, though, I probably wouldn't be writing this now. Most of my suit was charred through to the inside layer. Even parts of my Nomex underwear were charred. But it never got all the way through to my skin.

I learned some good lessons from that experience. I now make sure I always put on dry gloves that have a Nomex lining, and I wear a double-layer balaclava that I tuck properly into my suit.

Miscellaneous Driver's Equipment

In addition to your helmet and driver's suit, you require other equipment: driving shoes, fire-retardant gloves, balaclava, underwear, and socks. Again, the same rule applies: buy the best and then take care of it.

Wearing fire-retardant underwear under your suit is absolutely critical as far as I'm concerned. A two-layer suit with underwear provides better protection than a three-layer suit without underwear. I know it's tempting not to wear it on hot days, but once you're in the car and driving you'll never know if it's hotter or not. It's also more comfortable wearing underwear between you and the suit—it helps absorb the sweat better.

Only wear gloves with a full lining of fire-retardant material between your hands and the leather palm surface. Many gloves don't have this, they only have leather on the palms. Turn them inside out to be sure. Some race-sanctioning groups require that drivers' gloves have the fire-retardant lining, while others don't. Again, check the rule book, or better yet, only buy the good ones with a fire-retardant lining.

A two-layer balaclava is required by most rule books rather than the single-layer model. It's preferable to use one with two eye holes, as opposed to the large single hole. It may take a little time to get used to the two eye holes, but the extra protection is well worth it.

It's the same story with driving shoes. Buy real driving shoes, which usually have a fire-retardant lining. They offer a lot more protection, and are much more comfortable than just using bowling shoes or running shoes, as some drivers do. If you're going to drive formula-type cars, you probably won't be able to work the pedals properly in the tight confines of the foot area of the cockpit with anything other than real racing shoes.

You may want to use a neck collar (a good idea) and/or a helmet strap (a must on ovals). These not only help support your head from the heavy g-forces in the corners, reducing fatigue, but will make a big difference if you're in a crash. Support for your neck and head in a crash is crucial.

James Weaver says: "Use the thickest gloves you can get. After all, you put your hands into the flames to undo your belts, get out, etc. I have mine custom-made. I also have my own balaclava made with the smallest eye openings possible, and a hole for radio lead and drink tube built in. Head and neck injuries are the worst. Make sure you have a padded headrest and that your head can't go back past vertical."

One other thing I feel should be mandatory: ear plugs. Not only will they save your hearing over the years, but they allow you to actually hear the car sounds better, concentrate better, and they mean you won't fatigue as quickly. Auditory input is important feedback when driving. If your hearing is impaired, you won't be as sensitive to what the car is telling you. The best ear plugs are the ones custom-molded to fit your ears, although the small foam ones work quite well for most situations.

Safety Harness

The safety harnesses, or seatbelts, in a race car may be the most important safety component of all. Once again, use only the best belts and take care of them. After all, they're taking care of your life. They also help support your body in the cockpit so that you can drive most effectively.

All belts should be replaced or rewebbed at least every two years. They will seriously deteriorate, losing up to 80 percent of their effectiveness, simply by being exposed to weather and ultraviolet light. And anytime you've had a crash, replace or reweb them immediately, as they will have stretched and weakened. Also regularly check, clean, and lubricate (if necessary) the buckle mechanism.

Belts should be tight before you start driving. Make sure you can tighten at least the shoulder belts while driving. Often, they seem to loosen during the course of a race, and you may be surprised at how far they actually stretch in a crash, allowing your body to impact things you would never imagine.

Anti-submarine belts not only help you from sliding forward in a crash, they also help support your body under heavy braking. So make sure they are adjusted properly—snug and comfortable.

Practice getting the belts undone in a hurry—and getting out of the car quickly. This could be very valuable practice. Many cars are practically impossible to get out of quickly.

Dr. Brock Walker says, "Focus on seatbelt anchoring points. There is no conceivable way that seatbelt anchoring points should be the same for every driver."

Make sure the belts are mounted properly—securely and in the right position. Sometimes the shoulder belts are mounted too far apart, which would allow them to actually slip past your shoulders in a heavy impact. Have them mounted so that they help hold you down, as well as keep you from being thrown forward in a crash.

Chapter 27

The Real Winner

A uto racing is no different than business or life. It provides the same ups and downs, the thrill of victory and the agony of defeat, the same lessons and emotions—good and bad—that each of us face in real life. Often, though, racing provides as many of these in one season as many people experience in a lifetime.

If you keep your eyes open—and your mind—you can learn many valuable lessons that will assist you in other aspects of your life. Remember this when your racing program is not going as well as you would like. There is more to racing than what you do on the track. It's how you use what you learn on the track in your everyday life that makes you a real winner.

Through racing I have met and become friends with many of the most genuine, interesting, and exciting people in the world. I have visited places that I never would have had I not raced. I have had the most rewarding and memorable experiences.

And finally, racing has helped make me a more complete person. It has encouraged me to be a team player, it has taught me how to work with and motivate people, to learn about business, engineering, advertising, and marketing. It has helped me to be a good money manager, to improve my public speaking, and, I hope, to be a good teacher and writer.

Appendix A

Speed Secrets

#1 The less you do with the controls, the less chance of error.

#2 The slower you move, the faster the car moves.

#3 Squeeze the brake pedal on, and ease off.

#4 The throttle is not an on-off switch.

#5 The less you turn the steering wheel, the faster you will go.

#6 Keep steering movement to a minimum.

#7 Check your mirrors as often as it takes to always know where everyone else is around you.

#8 A shift should be made gently and with finesse.

#9 Brake first—then downshift.

#10 You will never win a race without understanding how tires work.

#11 Drive at the lowest possible slip angle that maintains maximum traction.

#12 Smooth is fast.

#13 Build up the tire's cornering force slowly.

#14 Overlap your braking, cornering, and acceleration forces.

#15 Races are won on the straightaway, not in the corners.

#16 It is better to go into a corner slow and come out fast, rather than vice versa.

#17 The more time you spend with the front wheels pointed straight ahead—or near straight—and the throttle to the floor, the faster you will be.

#18 The less time spent braking, the faster you'll be.

#19 Before you can win, you have to learn where to go fast.

#20 The most important corner is the fastest one leading onto a straightaway.

#21 Look for and drive the grippiest pavement.

#22 If the car feels like it is on rails, you are probably driving too slow.

#23 When passing, always "present" yourself.

#24 Focus on your own performance rather than on the competition.

#25 Focus your eyes where you want to go, not where you don't want to go or where you are.

#26 Look—and think—as far ahead as possible.

#27 Your right foot should either be on the brakes, squeezing the throttle down, or flat to the floor.

#28 Practice how you plan to race, and then you'll race as you practiced.

#29 Practice doesn't make perfect; only perfect practice makes perfect.

#30 Races are not won in the first corner; however, they are often lost there.

#31 Most races are decided in the last 10 percent of the race.

#32 You have to be close to take advantage of luck.

#33 Given equal cars and equal talent, the driver who is in the best physical condition is going to win.

#34 If you can't afford good safety equipment, you can't afford to go racing.

Appendix B

Recommended Reading

Motorsports Medicine, by Dr. Harlen Hunter and Rick Stoff, 1993, ISBN#0-9634819-0-8
This book describes how to design a training program that will help a race driver deal with the physical aspects of driving.

Race Car Engineering and Mechanics, by Paul Van Valkenburg, 1986, ISBN#0-9617425-0-X
The most readable and best overall explanation of vehicle dynamics available. Although written more for the engineer/mechanic than the driver, it is still very valuable. A must-read.

Prepare to Win by Carroll Smith, 1998, ISBN#0-87938-143-4
Tune to Win by Carroll Smith, 1980, ISBN#0-87938-071-3
Engineer to Win by Carroll Smith, 1984, ISBN#0-87938-186-8
These three books are must-reads for any driver who works on his/her own race car, and even for those who never touch a wrench, as they give a driver a good understanding of what is really going on with the car, and what it takes to prepare and maintain a race car.

Inside Racing Technology, by Paul Haney and Jeff Braun, 1995, ISBN#0-9646414-0-2
The best and most up-to-date information on the latest race technology, particularly shock absorbers. Another must-read for drivers.

Performance Handling, by Don Alexander, 1991, ISBN#0-87938-418-2
Although this book doesn't go into great detail on vehicle dynamics and handling, it is probably the easiest to understand.

Data Power: Using Racecar Data Acquisition, by Buddy Fey, 1993, ISBN#1-88109-601-7
In today's racing world, this book is a must-read, as it offers just about everything a driver will need to know about data acquisition.

Sponsorship and the World of Motor Racing, by Guy Edwards, 1993, out-of-print
This is the best book on the subject of motorsports sponsorship. If you have any interest in finding sponsors, keeping sponsors, and understanding how it all works, read this book.

How to Reach the Top as a Competition Driver, by Stuart Turner and John Taylor, 1991, ISBN#1-85260-378-X, out-of-print
This book is written more for the British or European racing scene, but the advice regarding the sacrifice and determination to reach the top is valuable and true for race drivers anywhere.

Unfair Advantage, by Mark Donohue with Paul Van Valkenburg
Although this book is a bit dated and hard to find, the information about how Mark Donohue developed his driving philosophy and techniques, the birth of the "traction circle," and the commitment he made to his career make it a good read.

Most of these titles are available from Classic Motorbooks (800-826-6600)

Index